365

Gardens

visit**Britain**™

Information
at your fingertips

When it comes to having a great day out, there's no finer place than England. This pocket guide is brimming with a wide selection of gardens that are open to the public, from Stowe's beautiful landscape gardens, to the 200-acre Lost Gardens of Heligan. England's world-famous parks and gardens are like little visions of paradise, places where man and nature combine to breathe life into beauty-inspired creations. Dip into this guide and you'll find 365 superb gardens, one for every day of the year!

The attractions in this guide are alphabetically ordered by county, and then by town. Some attractions will be accompanied by the following symbol:

The Quality Assured Visitor Attraction sign indicates that the attraction is assessed annually and meets the standards required to receive the quality marque.

Key to attraction facilities

☕	Café/restaurant
⛱	Picnic area
🐕	Dogs allowed
🚫🐕	No dogs except service dogs
♿	Full disabled access
♿ᴾ	Partial disabled access

For more information on attractions in England, visit enjoyengland.com.

How to use
this guide

Each visitor attraction contains the following essential information.

① ③ ④ ②

Exbury Gardens and
Steam Railway

Exbury Gardens and Steam Railway, Exbury Estate
Office, Exbury, SO45 1AZ   **t:** (023) 8089 1203
w: exbury.co.uk.

open: Apr-Nov, daily 1000-1730.
admission: £7.50

description: Over 200 acres of woodland
garden, including the Rothschild
collection of rhododendrons, azaleas, camellias and
magnolias. Enjoy our 12.25-inch narrow-gauge steam railway.

facilities: ⊓ 🐕 ⎴ ♿

⑦ ⑤ ⑥

1   Name
2   City/Town
3   Address and contact details
4   Opening times
5   Price of admission
6   Description
7   Facilities

Admission is free if the price is not specified. The price is based on a
single adult admission.

Please note, as changes often occur after press date, it is advisable
to confirm opening times and admission prices before travelling.

Swiss Garden

OLD WARDEN

The Swiss Garden, Old Warden Park, Old Warden, SG18 9ER
t: (01767) 627666 **w:** shuttleworth.org

open:	Apr-Oct, daily 1000-1700. Nov-Mar, daily 1000-1600.
admission:	£10.00
description:	A romantic and picturesque nine-acre garden. An outstanding example of the Swiss picturesque. Many fine specimens of shrubs and conifers, grotto, fernery, Indian Pavilion.
facilities:	

Wrest Park Gardens

SILSOE

Wrest Park Gardens, Silsoe, MK45 4HS
t: (01525) 860152 **w:** english-heritage.org.uk

open: Apr-Jun, Sat-Sun, Bank Hols 1000-1800. Jul-Aug, Mon, Thu-Sun 1000-1800. Sep, Sat-Sun 1000-1800. Oct, Sat-Sun 1000-1700.

admission:	£4.50
description:	One hundred and fifty years of English gardens laid out in the early 18thC including painted pavilion, Chinese bridge, lakes, classical temple, orangery and bath house.
facilities:	

Living Rainforest

NEWBURY

The Living Rainforest, Hampstead Norreys, Thatcham, Newbury, RG18 0TN **t:** (01635) 202444
w: livingrainforest.org

open:	Daily 1000-1715.
admission:	£6.00

description: Two tropical rainforests, all under cover, approximately 20,000 sq ft. Collection of rare and exotic tropical plants together with small representation of wildlife.

facilities: ♨ ⚒ ⛩ ♿

Waddesdon Manor

AYLESBURY

Waddesdon Manor, Waddesdon, Aylesbury,
HP18 0JH **t:** (01296) 653226 **w:** waddesdon.org.uk

open:	Gardens: Apr-Dec, Wed-Sun, Bank Hols 1000-1700. House: Apr-Oct, Wed-Fri, Bank Hols 1200-1600, Sat-Sun 1100-1600.
admission:	£15.00

description: A French Renaissance-style chateau housing the Rothschild Collection of art treasures, wine cellars, two licensed restaurants, gift and wine shops, an aviary and spectacular gardens.

facilities: ♨ ⚒ ⛩ ♿

Stowe Landscape Gardens

Stowe Landscape Gardens, The National Trust, Stowe
Landscape Gardens, Stowe, MK18 5EH
t: (01280) 822850   **w:** nationaltrust.org.uk/stowegardens

open:	1 Mar-4 Nov, Wed-Sun 1030-1730. 10 Nov-24 Feb, Sat-Sun 1030-1600. Gardens closed 26 May.
admission:	£6.00

description: Discover Stowe, a garden full of mystery and hidden meanings - one of Europe's most beautiful and influential landscape gardens. Perfect for a family picnic or for those seeking peace and tranquillity, with walks and trails for all to enjoy. Visit our web

facilities: ☕ 🐕 ⛱ ♿

Cliveden

Cliveden, Taplow, SL6 0JA
t: (01628) 605069   **w:** nationaltrust.org.uk

open:	House: Apr-Oct, Thu, Sun 1500-1730. Garden: Apr-Oct, daily 1100-1800. Nov-Dec, daily 1100-1600. Woodland: Apr-Oct, daily 1100-1730. Nov-Feb, daily 1100-1600.
admission:	£7.50
description:	Overlooking the Thames, the present house, built in 1851, was once the home of Lady Astor, and is situated in 375 acres of gardens, woodland and riverside walks.

facilities: ☕ 🐕 ♿

Cambridge University Botanic Garden

Cambridge University Botanic Garden, Cory Lodge, Bateman Street, Cambridge, CB2 1JF
t: (01223) 336265

open:	Daily 1000-1600.
admission:	£3.00

description: Forty-acre oasis of beautiful gardens and glasshouses, with some 80,000 plant species. Rock, winter and dry gardens, tropical glasshouse and lake. Unique systematic beds.

facilities: 🍺 🏃 ⛱ ♿

Anglesey Abbey, Gardens and Lode Mill

Anglesey Abbey, Gardens and Lode Mill, Quy Road, Lode, CB25 9EJ   **t:** (01223) 810080   **w:** nationaltrust.org.uk

open:	Abbey: Apr-Oct, Wed-Sun 1300-1700. Gardens: Apr-Oct, Wed-Sun 1030-1730. Lode Mill: Apr-Oct, Wed-Sun 1300-1700.
admission:	£8.80

description: A 13thC abbey with a later Jacobean-style house and the famous Fairhaven collection of paintings and furniture. There is also an outstanding 100-acre garden and arboretum.

facilities: 🍺 🏃 ⛱ ♿

Crossing House

Crossing House, 78 Meldreth Road, Shepreth, SG8 6PS
t: (01763) 261071

open:	Daily, dawn-dusk.
description:	The crossing-keeper's cottage and a small plantsman's garden with a very wide variety of plants.
facilities:	✗ ♿

Docwra's Manor Garden

Docwra's Manor Garden, 2 Meldreth Road, Shepreth, SG8 6PS   **t:** (01763) 261473
w: docwrasmanorgarden.co.uk

open:	All year, Wed-Fri 1000-1600.
admission:	£4.00
description:	Walled gardens round an 18thC redbrick house approached by 18thC wrought-iron gates. There are barns, a 20thC folly and unusual plants.
facilities:	✗

Little Moreton Hall (NT)

Little Moreton Hall (National Trust),
Congleton, CW12 4SD
t: (01260) 272018
w: nationaltrust.org.uk

open: Mar, Wed-Sun 1130-1600. Apr-Oct, Wed-Sun, 1130-1700. Nov, Sat-Sun 1130-1600.

admission: £5.50

description: A perfect example of a half-timbered moated manor house with Great Hall, Elizabethan long gallery and chapel. Elizabethan-style knot and herb garden.

facilities: ▬ ⚒ ⛺ ♿

Lyme Park (NT)

Lyme Park (National Trust), Disley, SK12 2NX
t: (01663) 762023   **w:** nationaltrust.org.uk

open: House: Apr-Oct, Mon-Tue, Fri-Sun 1300-1700. Park: Apr-Sep, daily 0800-2030. Oct-Feb, daily 0800-1800.

admission: £6.50

description: A National Trust country estate set in 1,377 acres of moorland, woodland and park. The magnificent house has 17 acres of historic gardens.

facilities: ▬ ⚒ ⛺ ♿

Tatton Park

Tatton Park, Knutsford, WA16 6QN
t: (01625) 534400   **w:** tattonpark.org.uk

open:	Parkland: Oct-Mar 1100-1700, last entry 1600. Apr-Sep 1000-1900, last entry 1800. Attractions: see website.
admission:	£5.00

description: Tatton Park is an impressive historic estate with 1000 acres of stunning deerpark to explore. Visit the Neo-Classical Mansion, 50-acre Gardens, Tudor Old Hall and working historical Farm. Also featuring speciality shops, restaurant, adventure playground a

facilities: ⬛ 🐕 🪑 ♿

Cholmondeley Castle Gardens

Cholmondeley Castle Gardens, Cholmondeley Castle, Malpas, SY14 8AH   **t:** (01829) 720383

open:	Apr-Sep, Wed-Thu, Sun 1130-1700.
admission:	£4.00
description:	Ornamental gardens, lakeside picnic area, a variety of farm animals including llamas. Tearoom and attractive gift shop. Ancient private chapel in the park. Plants for sale.

facilities: ⬛ 🐕 🪑 ♿

Ness Botanic Gardens

Ness Botanic Gardens, University of Liverpool, Ness, Neston, CH64 4AY   **t:** (0151) 353 0123
w: nessgardens.org.uk

open:	Feb-Oct, daily 0930-1700. Nov-Jan, daily 0930-1600.
admission:	£5.50
description:	The gardens contain a large collection of trees, shrubs, roses and heathers. Facilities include a visitor centre, tearoom, shop and plant nursery.

facilities: ⬛ 🏓 🅰 ♿

Arley Hall & Gardens

Arley Hall & Gardens, Northwich, CW9 6NA
t: (01565) 777353   **w:** arleyhallandgardens.com

open:	31 Mar-30 Sep 1100-1700. Hall open Tue, Sun and Bank Holidays only.
admission:	£5.00
description:	Rich in history and beauty, Arley offers award-winning gardens and a beautiful Victorian/Jacobean Hall. Marvel at the double herbaceous border, giant Ilex columns and explore the Victorian Rooftree and delightful woodland trails in the Grove.

facilities: ⬛ 🐕 🅰 ♿

Hare Hill

Hare Hill, Over Alderley, SK10 4QB
t: (01625) 584412   **w:** nationaltrust.org.uk

open:	Apr, Wed-Thu, Sat-Sun 1000-1700. May, daily 1000-1700. Jun-Oct, Wed-Thu, Sat-Sun 1000-1700.
admission:	£2.70
description:	A woodland garden with azaleas, rhododendrons and a delightful walled garden at its heart, containing a pergola and wire sculptures.
facilities:	⚒ ⎚ ♿

Capesthorne Hall

Capesthorne Hall, Siddington, SK11 9JY
t: (01625) 861221   **w:** capesthorne.com

open:	Apr-Oct, Wed, Sun, Bank Hols 1330-1600.
admission:	£4.00
description:	Sculptures, paintings, furniture and family monuments. A Georgian chapel, tearooms, gardens, lakes, nature walks and a touring caravan park.

facilities:	☕ ⚒ ♿

Walton Hall and Gardens

WARRINGTON

Walton Hall and Gardens, Walton Lea Road, Higher Walton, Warrington, WA4 6SN **t:** (01925) 261957
w: warrington.gov.uk/waltongardens

open:	Daily 0800-dusk.
description:	An ideal place for a family day out, with extensive lawns, picnic areas, ornamental gardens, woodland trails and a children's zoo.
facilities:	🍴 🐕 🪑 ♿

Penjerrick Garden

BUDOCK WATER

Penjerrick Garden, Budock Water, TR11 5ED **t:** (01872) 870105
w: penjerrickgarden.co.uk

open:	Mar-Sep, Wed, Fri, Sun, 1330-1630.
admission:	£2.50
description:	Spring flowering garden with camellias, rhododendrons, tree ferns, trees and ponds. Very tranquil, wild and non-commercial.
facilities:	🐕

Mount Edgcumbe House and Park

CREMYLL

Mount Edgcumbe House and Park, Cremyll, PL10 1HZ
t: (01752) 822236   **w:** mountedgcumbe.gov.uk

open:	Apr-Sep, Mon-Thu, Sun 1100-1630.
admission:	£4.50

description: Restored Tudor mansion, past home of Earl of Mount Edgcumbe. French, Italian and English formal gardens with temples and 800 acres of parkland.

facilities:

Trevarno

CROWNTOWN

Trevarno, Crowntown, TR13 0RU
t: (01326) 574274   **w:** trevarno.co.uk

open:	Daily 1030-1700.
admission:	£5.75

description: Do not miss a visit to the historic Trevarno Estate where you can explore the magnificent gardens, grounds and woodland walks which date back to 1246.

facilities:

Trelissick Garden

Trelissick Garden, Feock, TR3 6QL
t: (01872) 862090   **w:** nationaltrust.org.uk

open:	Apr-Oct. Mar, daily 1030-1730. Nov-Feb, daily 1100-1600.
admission:	£5.50
description:	Large garden, lovely in all seasons. Superb views of estuary and Falmouth harbour. Woodland walks beside the River Fal.
facilities:	🍵 🏃 ⛱ ♿

Caerhays Castle Gardens

Caerhays Castle Gardens, Caerhays, Gorran, PL26 6LY
t: (01872) 501310   **w:** caehays.co.uk

open:	Feb-May, daily 1000-1700.
admission:	£5.50
description:	A 60-acre woodland garden renowned for its collections of camellias, magnolias, rhododendrons and oaks.
facilities:	🍵 🏃 ⛱ ♿

Trewithen

Trewithen, Grampound Road, TR2 4DD
t: (01726) 883647   **w:** trewithengardens.co.uk

open:	Feb-May, daily 1000-1630. Jun-Sep, Mon-Sat 1000-1630.
admission:	£4.50

description: Gardens renowned for camellias, rhododendrons, magnolias and many rare plants. An 18thC landscaped parkland. House built in 1720. Audiovisual on history of Trewithen.

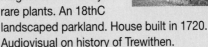

facilities: ▬ ⋏ ⊼ ♿

Burncoose Gardens and Nursery

Burncoose Gardens and Nursery, Gwennap, TR16 6BJ
t: (01209) 860316   **w:** burncoose.co.uk

open:	All year, Mon-Sat 0830-1700, Sun 1100-1700.
admission:	£2.00

description: A 30-acre woodland garden featuring rhododendrons, magnolias, azaleas and other ornamental trees and shrubs alongside a working nursery.

facilities: ▬ ⚒ ⊼ ♿

Trengwainton Garden

Trengwainton Garden, Madron, TR20 8RZ
t: (01736) 363148   **w:** nationaltrust.org.uk

open:	Feb-Oct, Mon-Thu, Sun 1000-1700.
admission:	£5.00
description:	Garden rich in exotic plants, views to Mount's Bay, stream and walled gardens with many plants which cannot be grown anywhere else on mainland UK.
facilities:	

Glendurgan Garden

Glendurgan Garden, Mawnan Smith, TR11 5JZ   **t:** (01326) 250906
w: nationaltrust.org.uk

open:	Mar-Oct, Tue-Sat 1030-1730.
admission:	£5.00
description:	A valley garden of great beauty, created in the 1820s and running down to the tiny village of Durgan and its beach. There are many fine trees and rare and exotic plants.
facilities:	

Trebah Garden

MAWNAN SMITH

Trebah Garden, Trebah, Mawnan Smith, TR11 5JZ
t: (01326) 250448 **w:** trebah-garden.co.uk

open: All year. Please see website for details.
admission: £6.50

description: A 26-acre ravine garden leading to private beach on Helford River. Extensive collection of rare and sub-tropical plants and trees. Water garden with koi carp.

facilities: ▆ 犬 冖 ᕐ

Lost Gardens of Heligan

PENTEWAN

The Lost Gardens of Heligan, Heligan, Pentewan, PL26 6EN
t: (01726) 845100 **w:** heligan.com

open: Mar-Oct, daily 1000-1800. Nov-Feb, daily 1000-1700.
admission: £8.50

description: The nation's favourite garden offers 200 glorious acres of exploration, which include extensive productive gardens and pleasure grounds, sustainably-managed farmland, wetlands, ancient woodlands and a pioneering wildlife conservation project.

facilities: ▆ 犬 冖 ᕐ

Eden Project

ST AUSTELL

Eden Project, Bodelva, St Austell, PL24 2SG
t: (01726) 811911 **w:** edenproject.com

open: Apr-Oct, daily 1000-1800. Nov-Mar, daily 1000-1630.
admission: £14.00

description: An unforgettable experience in a breathtaking epic location. A gateway into the fascinating world of plants and people.

facilities:

Pine Lodge Gardens & Nursery

ST AUSTELL

Pine Lodge Gardens & Nursery, Holmbush, St Austell, PL25 3RQ **t:** (01726) 73500 **w:** pine-lodge.co.uk

open: Daily 1000-1800.
admission: £5.50

description: Thirty acres with over 6,000 plants. Herbaceous and shrub borders, many water features. Lake with waterfowl and black swans. Plant-hunting expeditions every year.

facilities:

Antony Woodland Gardens and Woodland Walk

Antony Woodland Gardens and Woodland Walk, Nr Antony House, Antony Road, Torpoint, PL11 2QA
t: (01752) 812364   **w:** nationaltrust.org.uk

open:	Garden: Mar-Oct, Tue-Thu, Sat-Sun 1100-1730. House: Apr-May, Tue-Thu 1330-1730. Jun-Aug, Tue-Thu, Sun 1330-1730. Sep-Oct, Tue-Thu 1330-1730.
admission:	£5.50
description:	Woodland garden bordering the Lynher estuary containing fine shrubs, magnolias, camellias and rhododendrons set in a Humphrey Repton landscape. Further 50 acres of woods.
facilities:	🍴 ♿

Rydal Mount and Gardens

Rydal Mount and Gardens, Rydal, Ambleside, LA22 9LU
t: (015394) 33002   **w:** rydalmount.co.uk

open:	Apr-Oct, daily 0930-1700. Nov-Dec, Mon, Wed-Sun 0930-1700.
admission:	£5.00
description:	Wordsworth's best-loved home for 37 years. It was here that he wrote many of his poems. He became Poet Laureate to Queen Victoria at the age of 74.
facilities:	🐕

Stagshaw Gardens

Stagshaw Gardens, Stagshaw Lane, Ambleside, LA22 0HE
t: (015394) 46027   **w:** nationaltrust.org.uk

open:	Apr-Jun, daily 1000-1830.
admission:	£2.00

description: A woodland garden on a slope overlooking Lake Windermere. A superb collection of rhododendrons and azaleas blend perfectly under the hillside oaks.

facilities: ⚔

Holker Hall and Gardens

Holker Hall and Gardens, Cark-in-Cartmel, Grange-over-Sands, LA11 7PL   **t:** (015395) 58328
w: holker-hall.co.uk

open:	Gardens: Apr-Oct, Mon-Fri, Sun 1030-1730. Hall: Apr-Oct, Mon-Fri, Sun 1200-1600.
admission:	£9.25

description: Magnificent hall, award-winning gardens and museum - three attractions in one setting. There is also the Courtyard cafe, food hall and free parking.

facilities: 🍽 ⚔ ⛱ ♿

Levens Hall & Gardens

Levens Hall & Gardens, Levens, Kendal, LA8 0PD
t: (015395) 60321   w: levenshall.co.uk

open: Gardens: Apr-Sep, Mon-Thu, Sun 1000-1700. House: Apr-Sep, Mon-Thu, Sun 1200-1600.
admission: £9.50

description: Elizabethan mansion and world-famous topiary gardens designed by M Beaumont in 1694. Fountain garden and nuttery, licensed restaurant and gift shop.

facilities: ☕ 🏹 ♿

Sizergh Castle and Garden

Sizergh Castle and Garden, Sizergh, Kendal, LA8 8AE
t: (015395) 60951   w: nationaltrust.org.uk

open: Castle: Apr-Oct, Mon-Thu, Sun 1300-1700.
Garden: Apr-Oct, Mon-Thu, Sun 1100-1700.
admission: £6.20

description: Occupied by the Strickland family for over 760 years. View some of the finest Elizabethan carved overmantels, English and French furniture and Jacobite relics.

facilities: ☕ 🏹 ⛉

Mirehouse Historic House and Gardens

Mirehouse Historic House and Gardens, Underskiddaw, Keswick, CA12 4QE **t:** (01768) 772287 **w:** mirehouse.com

open:	House: Apr-Oct, Sun, Wed 1400-1700.
	Gardens: Apr-Oct, daily 1000-1700.
admission:	£2.60
description:	Family-run historic house with strong literary connections in a spectacular location. Four playgrounds, beautiful gardens and tearoom.
facilities:	💻 🍴

Acorn Bank Garden & Watermill

Acorn Bank Garden & Watermill, Temple Sowerby, Penrith, CA10 1SP **t:** (01768) 361893 **w:** nationaltrust.org.uk

open:	Mar-Oct, Wed-Sun 1000-1700.
admission:	£3.20
description:	Delightful sheltered garden, with a backdrop of a red sandstone 17thC house, renowned for its herbs and orchards growing old English fruit varieties. Over 200 culinary and medicinal herbs.
facilities:	💻 🐕 ⛩

Dalemain Historic House & Gardens

PENRITH

Dalemain Historic House & Gardens, Dalemain, Penrith,
CA11 0HB   **t:** (01768) 486450   **w:** dalemain.com

open:	Gardens: Apr-Oct, Mon-Thu, Sun 1030-1700. Nov-Mar, Mon-Thu, Sun 1100-1600. House: Apr-Oct, Mon-Thu, Sun 1115-1600.
admission:	£6.50
description:	A medieval, Tudor and early-Georgian house. Guided tours available. Wonderful five-acre plantsman garden set against the splendour of the Lakeland Fells.
facilities:	

Winderwath Gardens

PENRITH

Winderwath Gardens, Winderwath, Temple Sowerby, Penrith,
CA10 2AG   **t:** (01768) 88250

open:	Mar-Oct, Mon-Fri 1000-1600.
admission:	£3.00
description:	Mature gardens with herbaceous borders, alpines, pond with picnic area. Plants and second-hand garden tools for sale.
facilities:	

Muncaster Gardens

RAVENGLASS

Muncaster Gardens, Ravenglass, CA18 1RQ
t: (01229) 717614   **w:** muncaster.co.uk

open:	Feb-Dec, daily 1030-1800.
admission:	£7.00

description: Plants from all over the world, especially the Sino-Himalayan region, nestle in the wild splendour of over 70 acres of gardens, with the dramatic backdrop of the glorious Lakeland fells.

facilities:

Graythwaite Hall Gardens

ULVERSTON

Graythwaite Hall Gardens, Graythwaite, Ulverston, LA12 8BA
t: (015395) 31333   **w:** graythwaitehall.co.uk

open:	Apr-Aug, daily 1000-1800.
admission:	£3.00

description: A fine example of Thomas Mawson's architecture comprising Dutch garden, rose garden, spring-flowering shrubs and rhododendrons.

facilities:

Lake District Visitor Centre Brockhole

WINDERMERE

Lake District Visitor Centre at Brockhole, Windermere, LA23 1LJ t: (015394) 46601 w: lake-district.gov.uk

open: Gardens: Daily 1000-1700. House: Apr-Oct, daily 1000-1700.

description: Visitor centre with interactive exhibitions, thirty acres of Mawson gardens and grounds, adventure playground, shop and information centre. Lakeshore access for all.

facilities: � ♐ 冚 ㅕ

Chatsworth House, Garden, Farmyard & Adventure Playground

BAKEWELL

Chatsworth House, Garden, Farmyard & Adventure Playground, Chatsworth, Bakewell, DE45 1PP
t: (01246) 582204 w: chatsworth.org

open: House: Mar-Dec, daily 1100-1730. Garden: Mar-Dec, daily 1100-1800. Farmyard: Mar-Dec, daily 1030-1730.

admission: £11.00

description: Visitors to Chatsworth see more than 30 richly decorated rooms, the garden with fountains, a cascade and maze and the farmyard and adventure playground.

facilities: ▣ ⚒ ㅕ

Belper River Gardens

Belper River Gardens, Matlock Road, Belper, DE56 1BE
t: (01773) 841482   **w:** visitambervalley.com

open: Daily.

description: Beautiful gardens situated by the River
                 Derwent - 'The National Heritage Corridor' -
                 which flows through the county of Derbyshire.

facilities: 🐕 ⛱ ♿

Hardwick Hall

Hardwick Hall, Doe Lea, S44 5QJ
t: (01246) 850430
w: nationaltrust.org.uk

open: Apr-Oct, Wed-Thu, Sat-Sun 1200-
1630.

admission: £9.00

description: Elizabethan country house, gardens and
                 parkland, with outstanding collections of
                 furniture, tapestry and needlework.

facilities: 🍵 🍴 ⛱ ♿

Lea Gardens

Lea Gardens, Lea, DE4 5GH
t: (01629) 534380

open:	Apr-Jun, daily 1000-1730.
admission:	£3.50

description: A 3.5-acre garden of species and hybrid rhododendrons, azaleas and kalmias in woodland settings with picturesque walks, extensive rock gardens and plant sales.

facilities: ☕ 🐕 ♿

Melbourne Hall: Gardens and Visitor Centre

Melbourne Hall: Gardens and Visitor Centre, Melbourne, DE73 1EN **t:** (01332) 862502 **w:** melbournehall.com

open:	Hall: Aug, daily 1400-1630. Gardens: Apr-Sep, Wed, Sat-Sun, Bank Hols 1330-1730.
admission:	£3.50

description: Queen Victoria's Prime Minister, Lord Melbourne, lived here as did Byron's friend Lady Caroline Lamb. There are famous formal gardens and a visitor centre.

facilities: ☕ ✂ ♿

Herb Garden

The Herb Garden, Chesterfield Road, Hardstoft, Pilsley, S45 8AH   **t:** (01246) 854268

open:	Mar-Sep, Wed-Sun, Bank Hols 1000-1700.
admission:	£1.50

description: A herb garden with containerised herb plants of 200 varieties on sale; selling pot pourri, herbal oils, scented gifts and a small selection of locally produced crafts.

facilities: 🐕 ♿

Renishaw Hall: Gardens, Arts Centre and Museum

Renishaw Hall: Gardens, Arts Centre and Museum, Renishaw Park, Renishaw, S21 3WB   **t:** (01246) 432310
w: sitwell.co.uk

open:	Apr-Sep, Thu-Sun, Bank Hols 1030-1630.
admission:	£5.00

description: Italianate gardens with terraces, statues, yew hedges and pyramids. The garden, park and lake were the creation of Sir George Sitwell. Arts centre and museum in Georgian stables.

facilities: 🍴 👪 ⛱ ♿

Bluebell Arboretum

BlueBell Arboretum, Annwell Lane, Smisby, LE65 2TA
t: (01530) 413700   **w:** bluebellnursery.com

open:	Mar-Oct, Mon-Sat 0900-1700, Sun 1030-1630. Nov-Feb, Mon-Sat 0900-1600.
admission:	£2.50
description:	Thriving young arboretum and woodland garden established in 1992, containing a large selection of beautiful rare trees, with many species planted for their autumn colour.
facilities:	✕ ♿

Calke Abbey, Park and Gardens

Calke Abbey, Park and Gardens, Ticknall, DE73 1LE
t: (01332) 863822   **w:** nationaltrust.org.uk

open: House: Mar-Oct, Mon-Wed, Sat-Sun 1230-1700. Garden: Apr-Oct, Mon-Wed, Sat-Sun 1100-1700. Jul-Aug, daily 1100-1700.
admission: £8.00

description:	Built 1701-1703, and largely unchanged in 100 years. Natural-history collections, 750 acres of park, ponds, trees, woodlands, walled gardens and pleasure gardens.
facilities:	▣ ✕ ⌂

Arlington Court

Arlington Court, Arlington, EX31 4LP
t: (01271) 850296
w: nationaltrust.org.uk

open: Mar-Oct, Mon-Fri, Sun 1030-1700.
admission: £7.00

description: Historic house with interesting collection.
Gardens with rhododendrons, azaleas and
hydrangeas. Carriage collection and rides.
Extensive estate walks.

facilities: ☕ 🏃 🪑 ♿

Pecorama Pleasure Gardens and Exhibition

Pecorama Pleasure Gardens and Exhibition,
Underleys, Beer, EX12 3NA   **t:** (01297) 21542
w: peco-uk.com

open: Apr-May, Mon-Sat 1000-1730. May-Sep, daily
1000-1730. Sep-Oct, Mon-Sat 1000-1730.
admission: £5.75

description: Spectacular Millennium Celebration Gardens,
passenger-carrying miniature railway with
steam and diesel locomotives, Peco Model
Railway exhibition, shop and play areas.

facilities: ☕ 🏃 🪑 ♿

Killerton House and Garden

Killerton House and Garden, Broadclyst, EX5 3LE
t: (01392) 881345   **w:** nationaltrust.org.uk

open: See website for details.
admission: £5.80

description: An 18thC house built for
                   the Acland family. Hillside
                   garden of 18 acres with
                   rare trees and shrubs.

facilities: ⬛ 🎿 ⛩ ♿

Garden House

The Garden House, Buckland Monachorum, PL20 7LQ
t: (01822) 854769   **w:** thegardenhouse.org.uk

open: Mar-Oct, daily 1030-1700.
admission: £5.50

description: Stunning, innovative planting centred on a
                   lovely walled garden surrounding the romantic
                   ruins of a medieval vicarage.

facilities: ⬛ 🎿 ♿

Bicton Park Botanical Gardens

Bicton Park Botanical Gardens, East Budleigh, Budleigh Salterton, EX9 7BJ   **t:** (01395) 568465
w: bictongardens.co.uk

open:	Apr-Oct, daily 1000-1800. Nov-Mar daily 1000-1700.
admission:	£6.95

description: Grade I Listed historical gardens featuring palm house, Italian and American gardens, indoor and outdoor play areas, shell house, museum, glass houses, garden centre, train ride.

facilities:

Lee Ford Gardens

Lee Ford Gardens, Lee Ford, Budleigh Salterton, EX9 7AJ
t: (01395) 445894   **w:** leeford.co.uk

open:	All year, Mon-Thu 1000-1600.
admission:	£4.00

description: Forty acres of parkland, formal and woodland gardens with extensive display of spring bulbs, camellias, rhododendrons, azaleas and magnolias. Adam pavilion.

facilities:

Mythic Garden Sculpture Exhibition

The Mythic Garden Sculpture Exhibition, Stone Farm, Chagford, TQ13 8JU   **t:** (01647) 231311
w: mythicgarden.com

open: Daily 1000-1700.
admission: £2.50

description: A five-acre landscaped arboretum and water garden with national collections of wild-origin birch and alder. Summer sculpture exhibition. Specialist tree nursery.

facilities: 🐕 ⛱ ♿

Escot Fantasy Gardens, Maze and Woodland

Escot Fantasy Gardens, Maze and Woodland, Escot Park, EX11 1LU   **t:** (01404) 822188   **w:** escot-devon.co.uk

open: All year, Mon-Sun 1000-1700.
admission: £5.50

description: Enjoy the natural historical gardens and fantasy woodland which surround the ancestral home of the Kennaway family. Here, in 220 acres of parkland, you'll find an arkful of animals with paths, trails and vistas.

facilities: ☕ 🐕 ⛱ ♿

Greenway

Greenway, Greenway Road, Galmpton, TQ5 0ES
t: (01803) 842382   **w:** nationaltrust.org.uk

open: Mar-Oct, Wed-Sat 1030-1700.
admission: £4.25

description: A glorious woodland garden in a tranquil setting on the banks of the River Dart. Renowned for rare half-hardy plants underplanted with native wild flowers.

facilities:

RHS Garden Rosemoor

RHS Garden Rosemoor, Great Torrington, EX38 8PH
t: (01805) 624067   **w:** rhs.org.uk/rosemoor

open: Apr-Sep, daily 1000-1800, Oct-Mar, daily 1000-1700.
admission: £6.00

description: Rosemoor, an enchanting 65-acre garden, offers year-round interest. Visit us for inspiration, tranquillity or simply a marvellous day out.

facilities:

Docton Mill and Gardens

Docton Mill and Gardens, Docton Mill, Spekes Valley, Hartland, EX39 6EA   **t:** (01237) 441369   **w:** doctonmill.co.uk

open:	Mar-Oct 1000-1800.
admission:	£4.00

description: Working watermill of Saxon origin. Eight acres of woodland, lawns and streams. Coastal waterfalls and beach within one mile of gardens.

facilities: 💻 🛖 🏖 ♿

Lukesland Gardens

Lukesland Gardens, Lukesland House, Ivybridge, PL21 0JF
t: (01752) 893390   **w:** lukesland.co.uk

open: Apr-Jun, Sun, Wed, Bank Hols 1400-1800. May, Sat, Sun, Wed, Bank Hols 1400-1800. 14 Oct-11 Nov, Sun, Wed 1100-1600.

admission: £4.00

description: A 24-acre garden, mainly trees, rhododendrons, camellias and magnolias. Bisected by a clear stream off Dartmoor. Many ponds, pools and waterfalls.

facilities: 💻 🐕 🏖 ♿

Coleton Fishacre House & Garden

Coleton Fishacre House & Garden, Brownstone Road,
Kingswear, TQ6 0EQ   **t:** (01803) 752466
w: nationaltrust.org.uk

open: Garden: Mar-Oct, Wed-Sun, Bank
Hols 1030-1700. House: Mar-Oct, Wed-
Sun, Bank Hols 1100-1630.
admission: £6.40

description: House and twenty-four acre garden in a
stream-fed valley set within the spectacular
scenery of the Heritage Coast. Created by
Lady Dorothy D'Oyly Carte between 1925 and
1940.

facilities:

Marwood Hill Gardens

Marwood Hill Gardens, Marwood Hill, Marwood, EX31 4EB
t: (01271) 342528   **w:** marwoodhillgarden.co.uk

open: Daily 0930-1730.
admission: £4.00

description: An 18-acre garden with three
small lakes, unusual trees
and shrubs, bog garden,
national collection of astilbes,
iris ensata and tulbaghias.

facilities:

Orchid Paradise

Orchid Paradise, Forches Cross, Newton Abbot, TQ12 6PZ
t: (01626) 352233   **w:** orchids.uk.com

open:	Daily 1000-1600.
admission:	£2.00

description: Orchid displays in bloom in natural setting. Orchid trees, other tropical foliage, rainforest pool and educational displays. All exhibits under cover.

facilities: 𝖷 &

Knightshayes Court

Knightshayes Court, Bolham, Tiverton, EX16 7RQ
t: (01884) 254665   **w:** nationaltrust.org.uk

open:	Mar-Nov, Mon-Thu, Sat-Sun 1100-1700.
admission:	£5.50

description: House built c1870 by William Burges. Celebrated garden features a water lily pool, topiary, fine specimen trees, formal terraces, spring bulbs and rare shrubs.

facilities: ▬ 𝖷 ⊼ &

Dartington Hall Gardens

Dartington Hall Gardens, Dartington, Totnes, TQ9 6EL
t: (01803) 862367   **w:** dartington.org

open:	See website for details.
admission:	£2.00

description: Medieval courtyard and Great Hall, landscaped gardens. The hall and gardens are part of a working environment and visitors are asked to respect the residents' privacy.

facilities: ▆ 𝄞 ♿

Abbotsbury Sub Tropical Gardens

Abbotsbury Sub Tropical Gardens, Bullers Way, Abbotsbury, DT3 4LA   **t:** (01305) 871387   **w:** abbotsbury-tourism.co.uk

open: Apr-Aug, daily 1000-1800. Sep-Oct, Feb-Mar, daily 1000-1700. Nov-Jan, daily 1000-1600.
admission: £8.00

description: Twenty acres of woodland valley. Exotic plants from all over the world, teahouse and gift shop, aviary and children's play area.

facilities: ▆ 𝄞 ⊓ ♿

Mapperton Gardens

Mapperton Gardens, Estate Office, Mapperton, Beaminster, DT8 3NR   **t:** (01308) 862645   **w:** mapperton.com

open:	Gardens: Mar-Oct, Mon-Fri, Sun 1100-1700. House: Jul, Mon-Fri 1400-1630.
admission:	£4.50
description:	Romantic valley gardens in unspoilt countryside, featuring Italianate garden, topiary, 17thC fish ponds and orangery. Marvellous Elizabethan manor house.
facilities:	☕ 🚶 ♿

Compton Acres

Compton Acres, 164 Canford Cliffs Road, Canford Cliffs, BH13 7ES
t: (01202) 700778
w: comptonacres.co.uk

open:	Mar-Oct, daily 0900-1800. Nov-Feb, daily 1000-1600.
admission:	£6.95
description:	Eleven distinct gardens of the world. The gardens include Italian, Japanese, water and rock garden and the new amateur-gardening garden.
facilities:	☕ 🚶 ♿

Forde Abbey and Gardens

Forde Abbey and Gardens, Chard, TA20 4LU
t: (01460) 221290   **w:** fordeabbey.co.uk

open: Abbey: Apr-Oct, Tue-Fri, Sun 1200-1600.
Gardens: daily, 1000-1630.

admission: £8.80

description: Founded 850 years ago, Forde Abbey was converted into a private house in 1649. Thirty acres of world-famous gardens, interesting plants and stunning vistas.

facilities: ▉ 🐕 🛆 ♿

Bennett's Water Gardens

Bennett's Water Gardens, Putton Lane, Chickerell, DT3 4AF
t: (01305) 785150   **w:** waterlily.co.uk

open: Apr-Sep, Tue-Fri, Sun, Bank Hols 1000-1700.

admission: £6.45

description: Eight acres of gardens. Outstanding displays of water lilies in summer. Monet-style bridge and gazebo. Nursery, gift shop and tearooms.

facilities: ▉ 🐕 ♿

Hardy's Cottage

Hardy's Cottage, Higher Bockhampton, DT2 8QJ
t: (01297) 561900   **w:** nationaltrust.org.uk

open: Apr-Oct, Mon-Thu, Sun 1100-1700.
admission: £3.50

description: Thomas Hardy was born here in 1840. It is
                 where he wrote 'Under the Greenwood Tree'
                 and 'Far from the Madding Crowd'.

facilities: 🐕 ♿

Kingston Maurward Gardens and Animal Park

Kingston Maurward Gardens and Animal Park, Kingston
Maurward College, Kingston Maurward, DT2 8PY
t: (01305) 215003   **w:** kmc.ac.uk

open: Jan-Dec, daily 1000-1730.
admission: £5.00

description: Set deep in Hardy's Dorset and listed by
                 English Heritage, these gardens include a
                 croquet lawn, rainbow beds and borders.

facilities: ☕ 🏃 ⛱ ♿

Minterne Gardens

Minterne Gardens, Minterne Magna, DT2 7AU
t: (01300) 341370   **w:** minterne.co.uk

open:	Mar-Oct, daily 1000-1800.
admission:	£4.00

description: Important rhododendron garden with many fine and rare trees, landscaped in the 18th century, with lakes,  cascades and streams. The setting of Great Hintock House in Hardy's 'The Woodlanders'.

facilities: 🏃 🏕

Moreton Gardens

Moreton Gardens, Moreton, DT2 8RF
t: (01929) 405084   **w:** moretondorset.co.uk

open:	Mar-Oct, daily 1000-1700. Nov-Feb, Sat-Sun 1000-1600.
admission:	£3.50

description: Moreton Gardens is a 3.5-acre landscaped garden in a beautiful south Dorset village associated with TE Lawrence (Lawrence of Arabia) who is buried in the adjacent churchyard. Plant centre. Ample parking.

facilities: ☕ 🏃 🏕 ♿

Knoll Gardens and Nursery

Knoll Gardens and Nursery, Stapehill Road, Hampreston, Wimborne Minster, BH21 7ND
t: (01202) 873931   **w:** knollgardens.co.uk

open: Feb-Dec, Wed-Sun, Bank Hols 1000-1700. May-Oct, Tue-Sun, Bank Hols 1000-1700.
admission: £4.50

description: One of the country's most extensive collections of grasses can be found within Knoll's informal English setting. The four-acre show garden, also featuring perennials, is the winner of six consecutive Chelsea Flower Show Gold Awards.

facilities: ⬛ 🏹 ♿

Crook Hall and Gardens

Crook Hall and Gardens, Sidegate, DURHAM, DH1 5SZ
t: (0191) 384 8028   **w:** crookhallgardens.co.uk

open: See website for details.
admission: £4.50

description: Medieval hall with Jacobean drawing room, turret and gallery, set in four acres of gardens. Two walled gardens, maze, silver and white garden and Shakespeare garden.

facilities: ⬛ 🏹 🪑 ♿

Houghall College

Houghall College, East Durham and Houghall Community
College, Houghall, Durham, DH1 3SG
t: (0191) 375 4700   **w:** edhcc.ac.uk

open: Daily 1000-1600.

description: Extensive gardens used as a horticultural
training resource by Houghall College.
Features include glasshouses, woodland
garden, general display gardens and the newly
opened 'The World of Trees' arboretum.

facilities: ▬ 𝕏 ⊼ &

University of Durham Botanic Garden

University of Durham Botanic Garden, Hollingside Lane,
Durham, DH1 3TN   **t:** (0191) 334 5521
w: dur.ac.uk/botanic.garden/

open: Apr-Oct, daily 1000-1700. Nov-Feb, daily
1100-1600.
admission: £2.00

description: A botanic garden set in
countryside and mature
woodland. There are plants
from North America, Himalayas
and China as well as rainforest
and desert plants. Also a
Mediterranean conservatory.

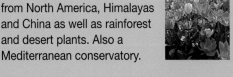

facilities: ▬ 𝕏 ⊼ &

Eggleston Hall Gardens

Eggleston Hall Gardens, Garden
Cottage, Eggleston,
DL12 0AG   **t:** (01833) 650115
w: egglestonhallgardens.co.uk

open:	All year, Mon-Sun, Bank Hols 1000-1700.
admission:	£1.00

description: Old established gardens growing many
species of plants. Vegetable garden with
organically grown vegetables for sale in
season. Also trees, shrubs, hardy perennials
and herbs.

facilities: ♨ ✗ ⊼ ♿

Burn Valley Gardens

Burn Valley Gardens, Hartlepool, TS25 5QS
t: (01429) 523421

open: Daily, dawn-dusk.

description: Opened in 1898, the gardens provide the
town's central green belt area. Children's
playground and bowls. A walkway takes you
through the family wood, on to Ward Jackson
Park.

facilities: ✗ ⊼ ♿

Burnby Hall Gardens and Museum Trust

POCKLINGTON

Burnby Hall Gardens and Museum Trust, The Balk, Pocklington, YO42 2QE   **t:** (01377) 288359
w: burnbyhallgardens.co.uk

open:	Apr-Sep, daily 1000-1800.
admission:	£3.75

description: Yorkshire in Bloom winner. The gardens are a glorious haven of beauty and tranquillity and include the two lakes that house the National Collection of hardy water lilies.

facilities:

Wassand Hall, Gardens & Grounds

SEATON

Wassand Hall, Gardens & Grounds, Seaton, HU11 5RJ
t: (01964) 534488   **w:** wassand.co.uk

open:	See website for details.
admission:	£5.00

description: A fine Regency house in beautiful tranquil surroundings, containing 18thC and 19thC paintings and a collection of English and European silver, furniture and porcelain from the same period.

facilities:

Sewerby Hall and Gardens

Sewerby Hall and Gardens, Church Lane, Sewerby, YO15 1EA   **t:** (01262) 673769   **w:** bridlington.net/sewerby

open: Hall: Apr-Oct, daily 1000-1700. Gardens: Daily, dawn-dusk.
admission: £3.80

description: Situated in a dramatic cliff-top position, forming the gateway to the Flamborough Heritage Coast, Sewerby Hall and Gardens, set in 50 acres of early 19thC parkland, enjoys spectacular views over Bridlington.

facilities: 🍴 🐕 ⛱ ♿

Sledmere House

Sledmere House, Sledmere, YO25 3XG
t: (01377) 236637

open: May, Tue-Thu, Sun 1100-1700. Jun-Aug, Tue-Fri, Sun, Bank Hols 1100-1700. Sep, Tue-Thu, Sun 1100-1700.
admission: £6.00

description: Georgian house containing Chippendale, Sheraton and French furnishing and many fine pictures. Magnificent plasterwork by Joseph Rose (Adam style). Capability Brown parkland, woodland walks, rose and knot gardens, chapel.

facilities: 🍴 🐕 ⛱ ♿

Gardens of King John's Lodge

ETCHINGHAM

The Gardens of King John's Lodge, King John's Lodge,
Sheepstreet Lane, Etchingham, TN1 7AZ
t: (01580) 819232   **w:** kingjohnslodge.co.uk

open:	Apr-Oct, please phone for details.
admission:	£3.00
description:	Beautiful romantic five-acre garden. Wild and secret gardens. Borders, water features, parkland. Nursery. Formal garden surrounding historic house. Orchards surround medieval barn.
facilities:	犬 丙 ♿

Gardens and Grounds of Herstmonceux Castle

HERSTMONCEUX

Gardens and Grounds of Herstmonceux Castle,
Herstmonceux, BN27 1RN   **t:** (01323) 833816
w: herstmonceux-castle.com

open:	Apr-Sep, daily, 1000-1800. Oct, daily 1000-1700.
admission:	£5.00
description:	Visitors can explore the Elizabethan walled garden, flower gardens and nature trail surrounding the castle. Children can enjoy the woodland play area.
facilities:	💻 犬 ♿

Merriments Gardens

HURST GREEN

Merriments Gardens, Hawkhurst Road, Hurst Green, TN19 7RA   **t:** (01580) 860666   **w:** merriments.co.uk

open: All year, Mon-Sat 1000-1730, Sun 1030-1730.

admission: £4.00

description: A four-acre garden featuring herbaceous borders, unusual plants, colour-themed borders, and a hidden stream which links two large ponds, a bog garden and a rock garden.

facilities: ⬛ 🎯 ♿

Sheffield Park Garden

SHEFFIELD PARK

Sheffield Park Garden, Sheffield Park, TN22 3QX   **t:** (01825) 790231
w: nationaltrust.org.uk

open: Apr, Jun-Sep, Tue-Sun 1030-1730. May, Oct-Nov, daily 1030-1730. Dec, Tue-Sun 1030-1600. Jan-Feb, Sat-Sun 1030-1600.

admission: £7.00

description: Capability Brown-designed landscaped gardens and woodland of 120 acres with four lakes on different levels. Noted for its rhododendrons, azaleas, rare shrubs and trees.

facilities: ⬛ 🎯 ⛱ ♿

Pashley Manor Gardens

Pashley Manor Gardens, Pashley Manor, Ticehurst, TN5 7HE
t: (01580) 200888   **w:** pashleymanorgardens.com

open:	Apr-Sep, Tue-Thu, Sat, Bank Hols 1100-1700. Oct, Mon-Fri 1000-1600.
admission:	£6.50
description:	Offers a blend of romantic landscaping, imaginative plantings and fine old trees, fountains, springs and large ponds. An English garden of a very individual character.
facilities:	⬛ 🐕 ⛱ ♿

BBC Essex Garden

BBC Essex Garden, Ongar Road, Abridge, RM4 1AA
t: (01708) 688479

open:	Apr-Oct, daily 0900-1730. Nov-Mar, daily 0930-1700.
description:	Garden with lawn, borders, small vegetable area, linked to Ken Crowther's BBC programme 'Down to Earth'. Also farmyard pets, tea shop, superb plants and clematis on sale.
facilities:	⬛ 🐕 ⛱ ♿

Green Island Garden

ARDLEIGH

Green Island Garden, Green Island, Park Road, Ardleigh, CO7 7SP   **t:** (01206) 230455   **w:** greenislandgardens.co.uk

open:	Apr-Oct, Wed-Thu, Sun, Bank Hols 1000-1700.
admission:	£3.00
description:	Beautiful gardens situated in 19 acres of woodland with a huge variety of unusual plants and lots of interest all year.
facilities:	▆ ⚔ ⊼ ♿

Roundwood Garden & Visitor Centre

BOCKING

Roundwood Garden & Visitor Centre, Bocking Church Street, Bocking, CM7 5LJ   **t:** (01376) 551728

open:	All year, Mon-Fri 0930-1630.
description:	Set in seven acres, delightful area for afternoon tea in the tearooms. Unusual plants and crafts for sale all year round. A visitors centre with conservation as its theme.
facilities:	▆ ⊼ ♿

RHS Garden Hyde Hall

CHELMSFORD

RHS Garden Hyde Hall, Buckhatch Lane, Rettendon, Chelmsford, CM3 8ET   **t:** (01245) 400256
w: rhs.org.uk

open:	Apr-Sep, daily 1000-1800. Oct-Mar, daily 1000-dusk.
admission:	£5.00

description: A 28-acre garden with all-year-round interest including a dry garden, roses, flowering shrubs, ponds, perennial borders and alpines.

facilities:

Marks Hall Garden and Arboretum

COGGESHALL

Marks Hall Garden and Arboretum, The Thomas Phillips Price Trust, Estate Office, Marks Hall, Coggeshall, CO6 1TG
t: (01376) 563796   **w:** markshall.org.uk

open:	Apr-Oct, Tue-Sun 1030-1700. Nov-Mar, Fri-Sun 1030-dusk.
admission:	£3.00

description: Garden and arboretum for every season of the year. Visitor centre with tea shop, information and gift shop. Admission £4.00 per car.

facilities:

Gnome Magic

DEDHAM

Gnome Magic, New Dawn, Old Ipswich Road, Dedham,
CO7 6HU   **t:** (01206) 231390   **w:** gnomemagic.co.uk

open: All year, Wed-Sun, Bank Hols 1000-1730.
admission: £4.00

description: An unusual treat, with a delightful garden and an amazing wood where gnomes and their friends live. Come and meet them.

facilities:

Beth Chatto Gardens Ltd

ELMSTEAD MARKET

The Beth Chatto Gardens, Elmstead Market,
CO7 7DB   **t:** (01206) 822007   **w:** bethchatto.co.uk

open: Apr-Oct, Mon-Sat 0900-1700. Nov-Mar, Mon-Fri 0900-1600.
admission: £4.50

description: Drought-tolerant plants furnish the gravel garden throughout the year, the dappled wood garden is filled with shade lovers, while the water garden fills the spring-fed hollow.

facilities:

Feeringbury Manor

Feeringbury Manor, Feering, CO5 9RB
t: (01376) 561946   **w:** ngs.org.uk

open:	Apr-Jul, Sep, Thu-Fri 0800-1600.
admission:	£3.00

description: A well-designed ten-acre garden, intensively planted with many rare and interesting plants for both dry and damp areas.

facilities: 🐕 ⛱ ♿

Gardens of Easton Lodge

The Gardens of Easton Lodge, Warwick House, Easton Lodge, Great Dunmow, CM6 2BB   **t:** (01371) 876979
w: eastonlodge.co.uk

open:	Apr-Oct, Fri-Sun, Bank Hols 1200-dusk.
admission:	£4.20

description: Twenty-three acres of beautiful historic gardens famous for their peaceful atmosphere. Featuring the splendid formal gardens created by leading Edwardian designer Harold Peto.

facilities: ☕ 🐕 ⛱ ♿

Gibberd Garden

The Gibberd Garden, Marsh Lane, Gilden Way, Harlow, CM17 0NA   **t:** (01279) 442112   **w:** thegibberdgarden.co.uk

open:	Apr-Sep, Wed, Sat-Sun, Bank Hols 1400-1600.
admission:	£4.00
description:	Important 20thC garden designed by Sir Frederick Gibberd, master planner for Harlow New Town. With some 50 sculptures.
facilities:	▣ 🎿 ⛱ ♿

Little Easton Manor and Barn Theatre

Little Easton Manor and Barn Theatre, Park Road, Little Easton, CM6 2JN   **t:** (01371) 872857

open:	Please phone for details.
admission:	£6.50
description:	Little Easton Manor has gardens, lakes and fountains. Also featuring the Barn Theatre, angling, a caravan and rally site, and refreshments.
facilities:	🎿 ♿

Red House Visitor Centre

Red House Visitor Centre, School Road, Messing, CO5 9TH
t: (01621) 815219

open:	All year, Mon-Fri 0930-1600.
description:	Sensory and artists' gardens, pond, children's play area and junior farm. Coffee shop, plant and craft sales, picnic area and conference venue.
facilities:	☕ 🏹 ⛩ ♿

Batsford Arboretum

Batsford Arboretum, Batsford Park, Batsford, GL56 9QB
t: (01386) 701441   **w:** batsarb.co.uk

open:	Feb-Nov, daily 1000-1600. Dec-Jan, Mon-Tue, Thu-Sun 1000-1600.
admission:	£5.00
description:	Fifty-acre arboretum containing one of the largest private collections of rare trees in the country, most spectacular in spring and autumn. Falconry, nursery and tearooms.
facilities:	☕ 🐕 ⛩ ♿

Mill Dene Garden

Mill Dene Garden, Mill Dene, School Lane, Blockley,
GL56 9HU   **t:** (01386) 700457
w: milldenegarden.co.uk

open: Apr-Oct, Tue-Fri 1000-1730.
admission: £4.50

description: Cotswold garden surrounding a water mill with millpond, stream and grotto. Steep valley hides surprises of colour, views and planting ideas.

facilities:

Bonsai World of Cheltenham

Bonsai World of Cheltenham, Two Hedges Road,
Woodmancote, Cheltenham, GL52 9PT
t: (01242) 674389   **w:** bonsai-world.co.uk

open: All year, Mon-Wed, Fri-Sat 0900-1700, Sun 1000-1600.

description: One of the largest Bonsai collections in Gloucestershire.

facilities:

Hidcote Manor Garden (National Trust)

HIDCOTE BARTRIM

Hidcote Manor Garden (National Trust), Hidcote Bartrim, GL55 6LR **t:** (01386) 438333 **w:** nationaltrust.org.uk

open: Apr-Jun, Mon-Wed, Sat-Sun 1000-1800. Jul-Aug, Mon-Wed, Fri-Sun 1000-1800. Sep, Mon-Wed, Sat-Sun 1000-1800. Oct, Mon-Wed, Sat-Sun 1000-1700.

admission: £7.00

description: One of England's great gardens, famous for its rare trees and shrubs, outstanding herbaceous borders and unusual plants from all over the world.

facilities:

Lydney Park Gardens

LYDNEY

Lydney Park Gardens, Lydney, GL15 6BU
t: (01594) 842844

open: Apr, Wed, Sun, Bank Hols 1000-1700. May-Jun, daily 1000-1700.

admission: £4.00

description: Extensive rhododendron, azalea and flowering shrub gardens in Lakeland Valley with unique Roman temple site and museum.

facilities:

Sezincote House and Garden

Sezincote House and Garden, Nr Moreton-in-Marsh,
GL56 9AW **t:** (01386) 700444 **w:** sezincote.co.uk

open: Garden: Jan-Nov, Thur-Fri, Bank Holiday Mon 1400-1800. House: May-Jul, Sep, Thur-Fri 1430-1730.
admission: £6.00

description: Sezincote is a unique Indian house, built in 1805 in the Mogul style of Rajasthan. The garden, with its Hindu Temple, seven pools and Persian Paradise Garden, is one of the most remarkable examples of the Picturesque style in the UK.

facilities: ✗ ⊼ &

Painswick Rococo Garden Trust

Painswick Rococo Garden Trust, Painswick, GL6 6TH
t: (01452) 813204 **w:** rococogarden.co.uk

open: Jan-Dec, daily, Bank Hols 1100-1700.
admission: £5.00

description: Eighteenth-century Rococo garden, set in a hidden combe, with garden buildings, vistas and woodland paths.

facilities: ▣ ⵊ ⊼ &

Snowshill Manor (National Trust)

SNOWSHILL

Snowshill Manor (National Trust), Snowshill, WR12 7JU
t: (01386) 852410 **w:** nationaltrust.org.uk

open: House: Apr-Oct, Wed-Sun 1200-1700. Gardens: Apr-Oct. Wed-Sun 1100-1730.
admission: £7.30

description: Cotswold manorhouse with eclectic collection of craftsmanship and arts and crafts garden.

facilities:

Stanway Water Gardens

STANWAY

Stanway Water Gardens, Stanway, GL54 5PQ
t: (01386) 584469 **w:** stanwayfountain.co.uk

open: House and Fountain: Jun-Aug, Tue, Thu 1400-1700. Fountain only: Aug, Sat 1400-1700.
admission: £6.00

description: Golden-stoned Jacobean manorhouse with exquisite gatehouse set amid 20 acres of landscaped grounds. Important 14thC tythe barn. Tudor great hall with shuffleboard.

facilities:

Westbury Court Garden (National Trust)

Westbury Court Garden (National Trust),
Westbury-on-Severn, GL14 1PD
t: (01452) 760461
w: nationaltrust.org.uk

open: Mar-Jun, Wed-Sun 1000-1700. Jul-Aug, daily 1000-1700. Sep-Oct, Wed-Sun 1000-1700.

admission: £4.00

description: Formal water garden with canals and yew hedges laid out between 1696 and 1705.

facilities: ⚒ ⛩ ♿

Westonbirt Arboretum

Westonbirt Arboretum, Forest Enterprise, Westonbirt,
GL8 8QS **t:** (01666) 880220
w: forestry.gov.uk/westonbirt

open: All year, daily 0900-dusk.

admission: £5.00

description: Six-hundred acres with the finest collections of trees, beautiful spring flowers, stunning autumn colours and a wide range of events.

facilities: ☕ 🐕 ⛩ ♿

Westonbirt School, Gardens & House

Westonbirt School, Gardens & House, Westonbirt School, Westonbirt, GL8 8QG   t: (01666) 881338
w: westonbirt.gloucs.sch.uk

open:	Easter, Summer School Hols, Thu-Sun 1100-1630. Oct School Hols, Daily 1100-1630.
admission:	£3.50
description:	Exquisite gardens surrounding the splendid country seat of Robert Holford, the great Victorian collector of plants who founded Westonbirt Arboretum.
facilities:	▦ 🐕 🪑 ♿

Dunham Massey Hall Park and Garden (NT)

Dunham Massey Hall Park and Garden (National Trust), Altrincham, WA14 4SJ   t: (0161) 941 1025
w: thenationaltrust.org.uk

open:	House: Apr-Oct, Mon-Wed, Sat-Sun 1200-1700. Park: Apr-Oct, Daily 0900-1930. Nov-Feb, Daily 0900-1700.
admission:	£6.50
description:	An 18thC mansion in a 250-acre wooded deer park with furniture, paintings and silver. Also, a 25-acre informal garden with mature trees and waterside plantings.
facilities:	▦ ✕ 🪑 ♿

Fletcher Moss Park

Fletcher Moss Park, Millgate Lane, Didsbury, M20 2RZ
t: (0161) 434 1877
w: manchester.gov.uk/leisure/parks/south/fletcher.htm

open:	Daily, dawn-dusk.
description:	The park has retained many of its original features such as the rock and heather gardens and the orchid houses situated in the Parsonage Gardens adjacent to Fletcher Moss.
facilities:	

Fletcher Moss Botanical Gardens

Fletcher Moss Botanical Gardens, Millgate Lane, Didsbury, Manchester, M20 2SW   **t:** (0161) 434 1877
w: manchester.gov.uk/leisure/parks/south/fletcher.htm

open:	Daily, dawn-dusk.
description:	The botanical gardens feature an interesting rock garden with many uncommon alpines, bulbs, screes and marginal plants. Also five grass tennis courts and five shale tennis courts.
facilities:	

Clifton Country Park and Wet Earth Colliery

Clifton Country Park and Wet Earth Colliery, Clifton House Road, Swinton, Salford, M27 6NG   **t:** (0161) 793 4219
w: salford.gov.uk/countryparks.htm

open: Park: All year, daily. Visitor Centre: Apr-Oct, daily 1200-1700. Nov-Mar, please phone for details.

description: A haven for wildlife. The habitats include woodland, grassland, wetland, ponds and a lake. Ideal for walking, fishing, cycling, bird-watching and nature study.

facilities: 🐕 ⛱ ♿

Haigh Hall and Country Park

Haigh Hall and Country Park, Haigh, Wigan, WN2 1PE
t: (01942) 832895   **w:** haighhall.net

open: Daily.

description: Set in 350 acres of wood and parkland. Facilities include a model village, bouncy castle, play area, miniature railway, ladybird ride, mini-golf, craft gallery, information centre, gift shop and cafeteria.

facilities: 🛏 🐕 ⛱ ♿

Sir Harold Hillier Gardens

The Sir Harold Hillier Gardens, Jermyns Lane, Ampfield,
SO51 0QA   **t:** (01794) 368787   **w:** hilliergardens.org.uk

open:	Daily 1000-dusk.
admission:	£7.50

description: Established in 1953, this magnificent collection of over 42,000 trees and shrubs is one of the most important modern plant collections in the world.

facilities:

Walled Garden

The Walled Garden, Down Grange, off Pack Lane,
Basingstoke, RG22 4ET   **t:** (01256) 845408
w: basingstoke.gov.uk/leisure/outdoors/walledgarden

open: May-Sep, Mon-Sun 0900-1800. Oct-Apr, Mon-Sun 0900-1500.

description: Beautiful herbaceous borders and formal yew hedge backdrop. Wildlife pond, show allotments and bee hives. Picnic area with willow sculpture and ecological plantings. Paintings exhibited in bothy.

facilities:

Spinners

Spinners, Boldre, SO41 5QE
t: (01590) 673347

open:	Gardens: Apr-Sep, Tue-Sat 1000-1700. Nursery: All year, 1000-1700.
admission:	£2.50

description: Woodland garden with a wide selection of less common shrubs. Rhododendrons, azaleas, camellias interplanted with wide range of ground cover and choice shade plants. Also nursery.

facilities: 朱 芹 ᕋ

Hinton Ampner Garden

Hinton Ampner Garden, Hinton Ampner, Bramdean, SO24 0LA   **t:** (01962) 771305   **w:** nationaltrust.org.uk

open: Garden: Apr-Oct, Mon-Wed, Sat-Sun 1100-1700. House: Apr-Jul, Sep-Oct, Tue-Wed, Sun, Bank Hols 1300-1700. Aug, Tue-Wed, Sat-Sun, Bank Hols 1300-1700.

admission: £6.50

description: Splendid 20thC shrub garden offering delightful walks and unexpected vistas. House contains a fine collection of Regency furniture and Italian paintings.

facilities: ☕ 朱 芹 ᕋ

Exbury Gardens and Steam Railway

Exbury Gardens and Steam Railway, Exbury Estate Office, Exbury, SO45 1AZ   **t:** (023) 8089 1203
w: exbury.co.uk.

open: Apr-Nov, daily 1000-1730.
admission: £7.50

description: Over 200 acres of woodland garden, including the Rothschild collection of rhododendrons, azaleas, camellias and magnolias. Enjoy our 12.25-inch narrow-gauge steam railway.

facilities:　🐕 🅿 ♿

West Green House Garden

West Green House Garden, West Green House, Thackham's Lane, West Green, Hartley Wintney, RG27 8JB
t: (01252) 845582   **w:** westgreenhousegardens.co.uk

open:　Apr-Sep, Wed-Sun, Bank Hols 1100-1630.
admission:　£5.00

description:　Painstakingly restored Queen Anne house and 18thC gardens surrounded by a neo-classical park with lake, follies, monuments, a water feature and ornamental birdcages.

facilities:　🍴 🅿 ♿

Houghton Lodge Gardens

Houghton Lodge Gardens, Houghton, SO20 6LQ
t: (01264) 810502   **w:** houghtonlodge.co.uk

open: Apr-Oct, Mon-Tue, Thu-Sun 1000-1700.
admission: £5.00

description: Tranquil landscaped gardens (Grade II*
Listed house) surround 18thC 'Cottage
Ornee', overlooking River Test. Walled garden
with borders and fine
trees. House open by
appointment.

facilities: 🚶 ♿

Braxton Gardens

Braxton Gardens, Lymore Lane, Milford-on-Sea, SO41 0TX
t: (01590) 642008

open: Daily 1000-1700.

description: Beautiful gardens set around attractive
Victorian farm buildings. David Austin rose
garden. Plant centre, gift shop, tearoom and
garden-design service..

facilities: 🍴 🚶 🪑 ♿

Furzey Gardens

Furzey Gardens, School Lane, Minstead, SO43 7GL
t: (023) 8081 2464   **w:** furzey-gardens.org

open:	Gallery: Apr-Oct, daily 1000-1700. Gardens: Daily, dawn-dusk.
admission:	£4.50
description:	Eight acres of gardens. Gallery displaying local crafts and paintings, many by local people. Old forest cottage. Nursery shop. Children's play log houses, lake.

facilities:

Mottisfont Abbey Garden, House and Estate

Mottisfont Abbey Garden, House and Estate, Mottisfont, SO51 0LP   **t:** (01794) 340757   **w:** nationaltrust.org.uk

open: House: Apr-May, Sep-Oct, Mon-Wed, Sat-Sun, 1100-1700. Jun, daily 1100-1700. Jul, Mon-Thu, Sat-Sun 1100-1700. Garden: Apr-May, Sep-Oct, Mon-Wed, Sat-Sun 1100-1700. Jun, daily 1100-2030. Jul-Aug, Mon-Thu, Sat-Sun 1100-1700. Nov-Dec, Sat-Sun 1100-1600.

admission: £7.50

description: The garden, with its collection of old-fashioned roses, forms a superb setting for the 12thC priory.

facilities:

Queen Eleanor's Garden

Queen Eleanor's Garden, Great Hall, The Castle, Winchester,
SO23 8PJ   **t:** (01962) 846476
w: hants.gov.uk/discover/places/great-hall.html

open:	Apr-Oct, daily 1000-1700. Nov-Mar, daily 1000-1600.
description:	A reconstruction of a 13thC garden at Winchester Castle named after Queen Eleanor. Also Great Hall with King Arthur's Round Table.
facilities:	🏃 ♿

Abbey Dore Court Garden

Abbey Dore Court Garden, Abbey Dore, HR2 0AD
t: (01981) 240419   **w:** abbeydorecourt.co.uk

open:	All year, Tue, Thu, Sat-Sun, BankHols 1100-1730.
description:	Six-acre plant lovers' garden full of interesting trees, shrubs and herbaceous perennials.
facilities:	💻 🏃 ⛱ ♿

Garden at the Bannut

The Garden at the Bannut, Bringsty, Bromyard, WR6 5TA
t: (01885) 482206   **w:** bannut.co.uk

open:	Apr-Sep, Wed, Sat-Sun, Bank Hols 1230-1700.
admission:	£3.00
description:	Two and a half acres of gardens with many fascinating features including colour theme gardens, lawns, mixed borders, knot garden, heather gardens, refreshments and 'secret' garden.
facilities:	☕ 🏇 ♿

Shipley Gardens

Shipley Gardens, Shipley, Holme Lacy, HR2 6LS
t: (01432) 870356   **w:** shipleygardens.plus.com

open:	Apr-Oct, daily 1000-1800.
admission:	£3.00
description:	The gardens, created during the last 40 years, are set within 30 acres of mixed environmental habitats and are managed as a home for birds, insects, butterflies and small mammals.
facilities:	☕ 🏇 ♿

Hampton Court Gardens HOPE-UNDER-DINMORE

Hampton Court Gardens, Hope-under-Dinmore, HR6 0PN
t: (01568) 797777   **w:** hamptoncourt.org.uk

open:	Apr-Oct, Tue-Thu, Sat-Sun 1100-1700.
admission:	£5.00

description: Stunning organic gardens. Their design blends harmonious planting with innovative water features. Ornamental kitchen garden, flower gardens, waterfalls, follies and a maze.

facilities: ☕ ✕ ⛱ ♿

How Caple Court Gardens HOW CAPLE

How Caple Court Gardens, How Caple, HR1 4SX
t: (01989) 740626

open: Apr-Sep, Mar, daily 1000-1700.
admission: £3.00

description: Eleven-acre Edwardian gardens overlooking river Wye. Formal terrace gardens and sunken Florentine water garden.

facilities: ☕ ✕ ⛱

Hergest Croft Gardens

Hergest Croft Gardens, Kington, HR5 3EG
t: (01544) 230160   **w:** hergest.co.uk

open:	Apr-Oct, daily 1200-1730.
admission:	£5.50

description: Spring bulbs in March and April,
rhododendrons and azaleas in May and June,
roses and herbaceous borders in high summer
and spectacular autumn colour.

facilities: 💭 🐕 ♿

Ivy Croft Garden

Ivy Croft Garden, Ivy Croft, Ivington Green, Leominster,
HR6 0JN   **t:** (01568) 720344   **w:** ivycroft.freeserve.co.uk

open:	See website for details.
admission:	£2.50

description: Beautiful garden in peaceful country setting,
full of interesting plants, some of which are
available in our small nursery.

facilities: 💭 🍴 ⛩ ♿

Stockton Bury Gardens Ltd.

Stockton Bury Gardens, Stockton Bury, Kimbolton,
Leominster, HR6 0HB   **t:** (01568) 613432

open:	Apr-Oct, Wed-Sun, Bank Hols 1200-1700.
admission:	£4.00
description:	Gardens laid out in ancient setting in unspoiled countryside with fine views. Pigeon house, tithe barn, hop kilns, unusual plants for sale.
facilities:	■ 🕴 ♿

Bryan's Ground Garden

Bryan's Ground Garden, Bryan's Ground, Letchmoor Lane,
Stapleton, LD8 2LP   **t:** (01544) 260001
w: bryansground.co.uk

open:	May-Jun, Mon, Sun 1400-1700.
admission:	£2.50
description:	A formal Edwardian garden, restored and extensively developed since 1993, of nearly eight acres with a newly created five-acre arboretum.
facilities:	■ 🕴 🛏 ♿

Arrow Cottage Garden

Arrow Cottage Garden, Ledgemoor, Weobley, HR4 8RN
t: (01344) 622181   **w:** arrowcottagegarden.co.uk

open:	May-Aug, Fri-Sun 1100-1600.
admission:	£3.50

description: Set amidst an idyllic landscape in rural Herefordshire, this romantic two-acre garden combines formal design, follies and topiary with exuberant and imaginative planting.

facilities:

Benington Lordship Gardens

Benington Lordship Gardens, Benington, SG2 7BS
t: (01438) 869228   **w:** beningtonlordship.co.uk

open:	See website for details.
admission:	£3.50

description: Edwardian garden on historic site. Ornamental, vegetable and rose/water garden. Herbaceous borders, lakes and contemporary sculptures.

facilities:

Hatfield House

Hatfield House, Hatfield, AL9 5NQ
t: (01707) 287010   **w:** hatfield-house.co.uk

open:	Apr-Sep, Wed-Sun, Bank Hols 1200-1700.
admission:	£9.00

description: Magnificent Jacobean house, home of the Marquess of Salisbury. Exquisite gardens, model soldiers and park trails. Childhood home of Queen Elizabeth I.

facilities: 🏃 ♿

Knebworth House, Gardens and Park

Knebworth House, Gardens and Park, The Estate Office, Knebworth House, Knebworth, SG3 6PY
t: (01438) 812661   **w:** knebworthhouse.com

open:	See website for details.
admission:	£9.00

description: Tudor manor house, re-fashioned in the 19thC, housing a collection of manuscripts, portraits and Jacobean banquet hall. Formal gardens, parkland and adventure playground.

facilities: 💻 🏃 ♿

Chelsea Physic Garden

LONDON

Chelsea Physic Garden, Swan Walk, (off Royal Hospital Road), London, SW3 4HS **t:** (020) 7352 5646
w: chelseaphysicgarden.co.uk

open: Apr-Oct, Wed 1200-dusk, Thu-Fri 1200-1700, Sun 1200-1800. Last entry 30 mins before closing.
admission: £7.00

description: London's oldest botanic garden and best-kept secret - a magical 300-year-old oasis in the heart of the capital. Discover the myriad uses of plants via free guided tours with entertaining guides, enjoy refreshments at the garden's renowned tearoom, and bro

facilities:

Lavender and Lace

ARRETON

Lavender and Lace, Church Lane, Arreton, PO30 3AB
t: (01983) 528419 **w:** arretonbarns.co.uk

open: Winter: daily 1000-1600. Summer: daily 0930-1700.

description: Eight herbal theme gardens (scented, aromatic, physic, zodiac, Roman culinary, Tudor, floral, and modern culinary). Fun for all the family and large free car park.

facilities:

Osborne House

Osborne House, York Avenue, East Cowes, PO32 6JX
t: (01983) 200022   **w:** english-heritage.org.uk

open:	Apr-Sep, daily 1000-1800. Oct, daily 1000-1600. Nov-Mar, please phone for details.
admission:	£9.50
description:	Queen Victoria and Prince Albert's seaside holiday home. Swiss Cottage where royal children learnt cooking and gardening. Victorian carriage rides. Award-winning gardens. New visitor centre with exhibition and shop.

facilities: 🍴 🏖 ⛱ ♿

Mottistone Manor Garden

Mottistone Manor Garden, Mottistone, PO30 4ED
t: (01983) 741302   **w:** nationaltrust.org.uk

open:	Apr-Oct, Mon-Thu, Sun 1100-1730.
admission:	£3.30
description:	A formal terraced garden noted for its colourful herbaceous borders, grassy terraces planted with fruit trees and its sea views.

facilities: 🍴 🐕 ♿

Ventnor Botanic Garden and Visitor Centre

VENTNOR

Ventnor Botanic Garden and Visitor Centre, Undercliff Drive, Ventnor, PO38 1UL
t: (01983) 855397 **w:** botanic.co.uk

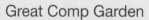

open: Gardens: Daily. Visitor Centre: Apr-Oct, Mar, daily 1000-1700. Nov-Feb, Sat-Sun 1000-1600.

description: Twenty-two acres of world themed gardens with a visitor centre, gift shop, cafe, two semi-permanent exhibitions and a plant sales area.

facilities:

Great Comp Garden

BOROUGH GREEN

Great Comp Garden, Comp Lane, Platt, Borough Green, TN15 8QS **t:** (01732) 886154 **w:** greatcomp.co.uk

open: Apr-Oct, daily 1100-1700.
admission: £4.00

description: A skilfully designed seven-acre garden with well-maintained lawns, a tree collection, shrubs, heathers, herbaceous plants, walls and terraces. Annual music festival.

facilities:

Marle Place Gardens and Gallery

BRENCHLEY

Marle Place Gardens and Gallery, Marle Place Road, Brenchley, TN12 7HS
t: (01892) 722304   **w:** marleplace.co.uk

open:	Apr-Oct, Mon, Fri-Sun 1000-1700.
admission:	£4.50

description: Romantic, peaceful, plantsman's gardens with topiary, unusual shrubs and plants, ponds, Edwardian rockery and Victorian gazebo. Walled scented garden and sculptures.

facilities: ☕ 🧗 ⛱ ♿

Beech Court Gardens

CHALLOCK

Beech Court Gardens, Beech Court, Canterbury Road, Challock, TN25 4DJ
t: (01233) 740735
w: beechcourtgardens.co.uk

open: Apr-Sep, Mon-Thu, Sat-Sun 1030-1730. Oct, Sat-Sun 1030-1730.

admission: £4.25

description: Informal woodland garden surrounding a medieval farmhouse. Fine collection of trees and shrubs, herbaceous borders and water garden. Meandering paths with surprising vistas.

facilities: ☕ 🧗 ⛱ ♿

Saint John's Jerusalem

St John's Jerusalem, Sutton at Hone, Dartford, DA4 9HQ
t: (01732) 810378   **w:** nationaltrust.org.uk

open:	Apr-Sep, Wed 1400-1800. Oct, Wed 1400-1600.
admission:	£2.00
description:	A large, tranquil garden moated by the River Darent around a former 13thC chapel, once part of a Knights Hospitaller Commandery church. Featuring magnificent trees and colourful herbaceous borders.
facilities:	

Doddington Place Gardens

Doddington Place Gardens, Doddington, ME9 0BB
t: (01795) 886101   **w:** doddington-place-gardens.co.uk

open:	Apr-Jun, Sun 1400-1700, Bank Hols 1100-1700.
admission:	£4.00
description:	Ten acres of landscaped gardens with formal sunken garden, Edwardian rock garden, fine trees, woodland, rhododendrons, azaleas, clipped yews and extensive lawns.
facilities:	

Brogdale Horticultural Trust

FAVERSHAM

Brogdale Horticultural Trust, Brogdale Road, Faversham, ME13 8XZ **t:** (01795) 535286 **w:** brogdale.org.uk

open:	Apr-Oct, daily 1000-1700. Nov-Feb, daily 1000-1630.
admission:	£5.50
description:	The National Fruit Collection has 4,000 varieties of fruit in 150 acres: apples, pears, cherries, plums, currants, quinces, medlars. Plant centre, tearoom and gift shop.
facilities:	� ▆ 🍴 ⛺ ♿

Bedgebury National Pinetum

GOUDHURST

Bedgebury National Pinetum, Park Lane, Goudhurst, TN17 2SL **t:** (01580) 211044 **w:** bedgeburypinetum.org.uk

open:	Daily 0800-1700.
admission:	£5.00
description:	A stunning, unique and internationally famous collection of conifers amidst beautifully landscaped lakes and avenues. Be amazed at the variety of colours, shapes and scents.
facilities:	▆ 🐕 ⛺ ♿

Groombridge Place Gardens and Enchanted Forest

GROOMBRIDGE

Groombridge Place Gardens and Enchanted Forest, Groombridge Asset Management Ltd, Groombridge, TN3 9QG   **t:** (01892) 861444   **w:** groombridge.co.uk

open: Apr-Nov, daily 1000-1730.
admission: £8.95

description: Winner of 'Best Tourism Experience' - Tourism Excellence Awards 2005. Gardens featuring traditional and 17thC walled gardens. In the ancient woodland of the Enchanted Forest there is mystery, innovation and excitement for all.

facilities:

Mount Ephraim Gardens

HERNHILL

Mount Ephraim Gardens, Hernhill, ME13 9TX
t: (01227) 751496   **w:** mountephraimgardens.co.uk

open: Apr-Sep, Wed-Thu, Sat-Sun 1300-1800, Bank Hols 1100-1800.
admission: £4.00

description: Fine herbaceous border, daffodils, rose terraces, topiary and a small lake. New water garden. Woodland area, orchard walk, Japanese style rock garden.

facilities:

Hever Castle and Gardens

Hever Castle and Gardens, Hever, TN8 7NG
t: (01732) 865224   **w:** hevercastle.co.uk

open:	Grounds: Apr-Nov, daily 1100-1800. Castle: Apr-Nov, daily 1200-1800.
admission:	£9.80
description:	A moated castle once the childhood home of Anne Boleyn. Restored by the Astor family, it contains furniture, paintings and panelling. Set in award-winning gardens.
facilities:	🍵 🐕 ⛱ ♿

Emmetts Garden

Emmetts Garden, Ide Hill, TN14 6AY
t: (01732) 868381   **w:** nationaltrust.org.uk

open: Apr-May, Tue-Sun 1100-1700. Jun, Wed-Sun 1100-1700. Jul-Oct, Wed, Sat-Sun 1100-1700.
admission: £5.50

description:	A shrub garden on a hillside with notable spring and autumn colours. Rare trees, shrubs and carpets of bluebells. Wonderful views over the Weald.
facilities:	🍵 🐕 ⛱ ♿

Scotney Castle
Garden and Estate

Scotney Castle Garden and Estate, Lamberhurst, TN3 8JN
t: (01892) 893868   **w:** nationaltrust.org.uk

open:	Garden: Apr-Oct, Wed-Sun 1100-1730. Nov-Dec, Sat-Sun 1100-1600. Estate: Daily.
admission:	£5.80

description:	Romantic gardens created around the ruins of a 14thC moated castle containing exhibitions. Gardens created by the Hussey family with shrubs, winding paths and superb views.

facilities:

Leeds Castle
and Gardens

Leeds Castle and Gardens, Broomfield, Maidstone,
ME17 1PL   **t:** (01622) 765400   **w:** leeds-castle.com

open:	Gardens: Daily 1000-1700. Castle: Daily 1030-1600.
admission:	£13.50

description:	A castle on two islands in a lake, dating from 9thC. Furniture, tapestries, art treasures, dog collar museum, gardens, duckery, aviaries, maze, grotto and vineyard.

facilities:

Penshurst Place and Gardens

Penshurst Place and Gardens, Penshurst, TN11 8DG
t: (01892) 870307   **w:** penshurstplace.com

open: Gardens: Apr-Oct, daily 1030-1800. House: Apr-Oct, daily 1200-1600.
admission: £7.50

description: A medieval manor house with Baron's Hall, portraits, tapestries, armour, park, lake, venture playground, toy museum and with Tudor gardens. Gift shop.

facilities: 🍵 ⚔ 🏕 ♿

Sissinghurst Castle Garden

Sissinghurst Castle Garden, Sissinghurst, TN17 2AB
t: (01580) 710701   **w:** nationaltrust.org.uk

open: Apr-Oct, Mon-Tue, Fri-Sun 1100-1830.
admission: £8.60

description: A garden created by Vita Sackville-West and Harold Nicolson around an Elizabethan mansion. A series of small enclosed compartments, intimate in scale and romantic in atmosphere.

facilities: 🍵 ⚔ 🏕 ♿

Pines Garden

The Pines Garden, Beach Road, St Margaret's Bay, CT15 6DZ   **t:** (01304) 851737   **w:** baytrust.org.uk

open:	Daily 1000-1700.
description:	Six acres of tranquillity. Mature trees, lawns, specimen shrubs, spring bulbs, lake, waterfall, grass labyrinth and rockery. Oscar Nemon's statue of Sir Winston Churchill.
facilities:	

Iden Croft Herbs & Walled Gardens

Iden Croft Herbs & Walled Gardens, Frittenden Road, Staplehurst, TN12 0DH   **t:** (01580) 891432
w: herbs-uk.com

open:	Apr-Sep, Mon-Sat 0900-1700, Sun, Bank Hols 1100-1700. Oct-Mar, Mon-Fri 0900-dusk.
admission:	£4.00
description:	Extensive aromatic herb gardens with walled garden and a variety of themed gardens demonstrating the beauty and use of herbs. National Collections of mentha and origanum.
facilities:	

Chartwell

Chartwell, Mapleton Road, Westerham, TN16 1PS
t: (01732) 868381 **w:** nationaltrust.org.uk

open:	Apr-Jun, Sep-Oct, Wed-Sun 1100-1700. Jul-Aug, Thu-Sun 1100-1700.
admission:	£10.80
description:	The home of Sir Winston Churchill with study, studio and museum rooms with gifts, uniforms and photos. Garden, Golden Rose walk, lakes and exhibition.
facilities:	🍵 🐕 ⛱ ♿

Squerryes Court Manor House and Gardens

Squerryes Court Manor House and Gardens, Westerham, TN16 1SJ
t: (01959) 562345 **w:** squerryes.co.uk

open:	Apr-Sep, Wed-Thu, Sun, Bank Hols 1130-1630.
admission:	£6.50
description:	Beautiful manor house, built 1681 containing tapestries, Old Master paintings, porcelain, furniture and items relating to General Wolfe. Gardens, lake, walks, and formal garden.
facilities:	🍵 🏃 ⛱ ♿

Goodnestone Park Gardens

Goodnestone Park Gardens, Wingham, CT3 1PL
t: (01304) 840107   **w:** goodnestoneparkgardens.co.uk

open:	Apr-Oct, Wed-Sat 1100-1700, Sun, Bank Hols 1200-1700.
admission:	£4.50
description:	A 14-acre garden with fine trees, a large collection of shrubs and old fashioned roses, walled garden, woodland garden, small arboretum and Jane Austen connections.
facilities:	☕ ⚔ 🛋 ♿

Yalding Organic Gardens

Yalding Organic Gardens, Benover Road, Yalding, ME18 6EX
t: (01622) 814650   **w:** hdra.org.uk

open:	Apr-Oct, Wed-Sun 1000-1700.
admission:	£4.00
description:	Five acres of stunning gardens - themed history displays, practical demonstrations of compost making and safe pest control. Cafe and shop.
facilities:	☕ ⚔ 🛋 ♿

Stanley Park

BLACKPOOL

Stanley Park, West Park Drive, Blackpool, FY3 9HQ
t: (01253) 478478   **w:** blackpool.com/sights/stanley.html

open: All year, Mon-Sun, Bank Hols dawn-dusk.

description: See the stone statues, formal borders and frothing fountains in the Italian gardens, meander along the pathways, and let the bridges carry you across the lake.

facilities:

Worden Park

LEYLAND

Worden Park, Worden Lane, Leyland, PR25 3EL
t: (01772) 625400   **w:** southribble.gov.uk/visitors

open: Daily 0800-1730.

description: The park is over 150 acres in size. It includes the formal gardens, overlooked by a magnificent conservatory originally built in 1892. Alongside is the famous maze or puzzle garden.

facilities:

University of Leicester: Botanic Gardens

University of Leicester: Botanic Gardens, The Knoll, Glebe
Road, Leicester, LE2 2LD   **t:** (0116) 271 7725
w: le.au.uk/botanicgarden/

open: Apr-Nov, daily 1000-1600. Dec-Mar, Mon-Fri
                 1000-1600.

description: Sixteen acres of rock, herb, water and formal
                 gardens with glasshouses organised for
                 teaching and research.

facilities: 🏃 ♿

Belton House, Park and Gardens

Belton House, Park and Gardens, Belton, NG32 2LS
t: (01476) 566116   **w:** nationaltrust.org.uk

open: House: Apr-Oct, Wed-Sun 1230-1700.
Park: Apr-Jul, Wed-Sun 1100-170. Aug, daily
1030-1730. Sep-Oct, Wed-Sun 1100-1730.
Garden: Apr-Jul, Wed-Sun 1100-1730. Aug, daily
1030-1730. Sep-Oct, Wed-Sun 1100-1730. Nov,
Fri-Sun 1200-1600. Feb, Sat-Sun 1200-1600.

admission: £9.00

description: Formal gardens, orangery and landscaped
                 park, built 1685-1688 for Sir John Brownlow,
                 with alterations by James Wyatt in 1777.

facilities: ▬ 🏃 ⛩ ♿

Candlesby Herbs

Candlesby Herbs, Cross Keys Cottage, Candlesby, PE23 5SF
t: (01754) 890211   **w:** candlesbyherbs.co.uk

open:	All year, Tue-Sun, Bank Hols 1000-1700.
description:	Specialists in the growing and usage of herbs with plants for sale and display, talks, lectures and demonstrations by arrangement, both on and off site.
facilities:	⚐ ♿

Elsham Hall Gardens and Country Park

Elsham Hall Gardens and Country Park,
Elsham Hall, Elsham, DN20 0QZ
t: (01652) 688698   **w:** elshamhall.co.uk

open:	Apr-Sep, Wed-Sun 1100-1700.
admission:	£5.00
description:	Elsham Hall Gardens and Country Park Arboretum. Animal farm, adventure playground, carp and trout lakes with carp feeding jetty and a wild butterfly garden and walkway.
facilities:	▣ ⚒ ⛩ ♿

Easton Walled Gardens

Easton Walled Gardens, Easton, Grantham, NG33 5AP
t: (01476) 530063   w: eastonwalledgardens.co.uk

open:	Apr-Sep, Wed, Fri, Sun, Bank Hols 1100-1600. Jul-Aug, Wed-Fri, Sun, Bank Hols 1100-1600. Oct-Dec, Sun 1100-1600.
admission:	£4.50

description: Twelve acres of gardens undergoing a major revival. Seasonal collections, garden walks, over 100 varieties of daffodil and popular cut-flower garden.

facilities: ▱ ⚔ 🛆 ♿

Doddington Hall

Doddington Hall & Gardens, Doddington, Lincoln, LN6 4RU   t: (01522) 694308   w: doddingtonhall.com

open:	Hall: May-Sep, Wed, Sun, Bank Hols 1300-1700. Gardens: May-Sep, Wed, Sun, Bank Hols 1200-1700.
admission:	£5.60

description: Superb Elizabethan mansion by the renowned architect Robert Smythson, standing today as it was completed in 1600 with walled courtyards, turrets, gatehouse. 6 acres of romantic garden.

facilities: ▱ ⚔ 🛆 ♿

Lincoln Arboretum

LINCOLN

Lincoln Arboretum, Monks Road, Lincoln, LN5 7AY **t:** (01522) 873423 **w:** lincoln.gov.uk

open: All year, Fri-Sat 0900-1700.

description: The Arboretum, one of Lincoln's most treasured parks, reopened in September 2003 following a £3 million restoration project to return the park to its former glory.

facilities:

Goltho House Garden and Nursery

MARKET RASEN

Goltho House Garden and Nursery, Goltho House, Lincoln Road, Goltho, Market Rasen, LN8 5NF
t: (01673) 857768 **w:** golthogardens.com

open: Apr-Sep, Wed, Sun 1000-1600.
admission: £3.00

description: A 4.5-acre garden and nursery including herbaceous borders, ponds, rose garden, nut walk, wild flower meadow, potager and much more.

facilities:

See pages 2-3 for key to symbols

Garden House

The Garden House, Cliff Road, Saxby, Market Rasen,
LN8 2DQ   **t:** (01673) 878820   **w:** thegardenhousesaxby.com

open:	May-Sep, Fri-Sat 1000-1700.
admission:	£3.00

description: A large garden with long terrace,
Mediterranean, Dutch, damp and dry gardens
with woodland, wildflower meadow, ponds,
spring bulbs.

facilities: 💺 🎿 ⛩ ♿

Rose Cottage Water Garden Centre Joinery, Spar and Bird Centre

Rose Cottage Water Garden Centre Joinery, Spar and Bird
Centre, Glenside North, Pinchbeck, PE11 3SD
t: (01775) 710882   **w:** rosecottagewgc.co.uk

open: Apr-Oct, Mon-Fri 0830-1700, Sat 0900-1700,
Sun 1000-1600. Nov-Mar, Mon-Fri 0830-1700,
Sat 1000-1600, Sun 1100-1500.

description: The UK's largest undercover display of spas
and spa buildings. Spa, hot tub and joinery
centre. Ponds, pumps, filters, and other
aquatic products. Water garden.

facilities: 🐕 ♿

Normanby Hall Country Park

SCUNTHORPE

Normanby Hall Country Park, Normanby, Scunthorpe,
DN15 9HU **t:** (01724) 720588
w: northlincs.gov.uk/normanby

open: Park: All year 0900-dusk. Hall: Apr-Sep, daily 1300-1700.

admission: £4.60

description: Winners of Yorkshire in Bloom 2001, 2003 and 2004. Whether you love gardens, wildlife or history, or just want a great day out with the family, Normanby is the place to be.

facilities:

Hall Place and Gardens

BEXLEY

Hall Place and Gardens, Hall Plac, Bourne Road, Bexley,
DA5 1PQ **t:** (01322) 526574 **w:** hallplaceandgardens.com

open: House: Apr-Oct, Mon-Sat 1000-1700, Sun, Bank Hols 1100-1700. Nov-Mar, Tue-Sat 1000-1615. Gardens: Daily, 0800-dusk.

description: Tudor house and award-winning gardens built for the Lord Mayor of London in the reign of Henry VIII in 1537.

facilities:

Syon Park Gardens

Syon Park Gardens, Syon Park, Brentford, TW8 8JF
t: (020) 8560 0882   **w:** syonpark.co.uk

open: Mar-Oct, daily 1030-1700. Nov-Feb, Sat-Sun 1030-1600.

admission: £4.00

description: Forty acres of gardens include the spectacular Great Conservatory, a rose garden and circular lakeside walk. The views across the Thames water meadows give Syon a unique rural aspect.

facilities: 🍵 ✕ ⛱ ♿

Forty Hall Museum and Gardens

Forty Hall Museum and Gardens, Forty Hill, Enfield, EN2 9HA
t: (020) 8363 8196   **w:** enfield.gov.uk/fortyhall

open: All year, Wed-Sun 1100-1600.

description: A Grade I Listed historic building housing local museum displays of 17thC and 18thC furniture and pictures. Set in parkland.

facilities: 🍵 ✕ ⛱ ♿

Myddelton House Gardens

Myddelton House Gardens, Bulls Cross, Enfield, EN2 9HG
t: (01992) 717711   **w:** leevalleypark.org.uk

open:	Apr-Sep, Mon-Fri 1000-1630, Sun 1200-1600, Bank Hols 1200-1600. Oct-Mar, Mon-Fri 1000-1500.
admission:	£2.60
description:	Gardens created by E A Bowles (1865-1954) featuring many unusual plants. Includes national collection of award-winning Bearded Iris.
facilities:	⚲ ⊼ ♿

Buddhapadipa Temple (Thai Temple)

Buddhapadipa Temple (Thai Temple), 14 Calonne Road, Wimbledon, London, SW19 5HJ   **t:** (020) 8946 1357
w: buddhapadipa.org

open: All year, Sat-Sun 0900-1800.

 **description:** A temple building in Thai architectural style featuring mural paintings and gardens. The original house is now the monks' residence.

facilities: ⚲ ♿

Carlyle's House

Carlyle's House, 24 Cheyne Row, London, SW3 5HL
t: (020) 7352 7087   **w:** nationaltrust.org.uk

open:	Apr-Oct, Wed-Fri 1400-1700, Sat-Sun 1100-1700.
admission:	£4.50
description:	This Queen Anne house was the home of historian, social writer and ethical thinker Thomas Carlyle and his wife Jane. The furniture, pictures, portraits and books are all still in place.
facilities:	🍴 🎋 ♿

Chiswick House

Chiswick House, Burlington Lane, London, W4 2RP
t: (020) 8995 0508   **w:** english-heritage.org.uk

open: Apr-Oct, Wed-Fri 1000-1700, Sat 1000-1400, Sun, Bank Hols 1000-1700.
admission: £4.90

description:	The celebrated villa of Lord Burlington with impressive grounds featuring Italianate garden with statues, temples, obelisks and urns.
facilities:	💺 🍴 🎋 ♿

Eltham Palace

Eltham Palace, Court Yard, London, SE9 5QE
t: (020) 8294 2548   **w:** english-heritage.org.uk

open:	Apr-Oct, Mon-Wed, Sun 1000-1700. Nov-Dec, Mon-Wed, Sun 1000-1600. Feb-Mar, Mon-Wed, Sun 1000-1600.
admission:	£7.60
description:	A spectacular fusion of 1930s Art Deco villa and magnificent 15thC Great Hall. Surrounded by period gardens.
facilities:	🍵 ♿

Jewel Tower

Jewel Tower, Abingdon Street, Westminster, London, SW1P 3JY   **t:** (020) 7222 2219   **w:** english-heritage.org.uk

open:	Apr-Oct, daily 1000-1700. Nov-Mar, daily 1000-1600.
admission:	£2.90
description:	One of only two original surviving buildings of the Palace of Westminster. Home today to 'Parliament Past and Present' - a fascinating account of the House of Lords and the House of Commons.
facilities:	♿

Kenwood House

LONDON

Kenwood House, Hampstead Lane, London, NW3 7JR **t:** (020) 8348 1286
w: english-heritage.org.uk

open: Apr-Oct, daily 1100-1700. Nov-Mar, daily 1100-1600.

description: A beautiful 18thC villa with fine interiors and a world-class collection of paintings. Also fabulous landscaped gardens and an award-winning restaurant.

facilities:

Museum of Fulham Palace

LONDON

Museum of Fulham Palace, Bishops Avenue, London, SW6 6EA **t:** (020) 7736 3233 **w:** fulhampalace.org

open: All year, Mon-Tue 1200-1600, Sat 1100-1400, Sun 1130-1530.

description: A historic building. Highlights include Tudor courtyard, 18thC walled garden, botanical collection and Museum of Fulham Palace. Tours include the Great Hall and Chapel.

facilities:

Museum of Garden History

Museum of Garden History,
Lambeth Palace Road, London,
SE1 7LB
t: (020) 7401 8865
w: museumgardenhistory.org

open: Daily 1030-1700.
admission: £3.00

description: The museum provides an insight into the development of gardening in the UK, with reproduction 17thC knot garden and collection of historic garden tools, ephemera and curiosities.

facilities: 💻 🧍 ♿

Morden Hall Park (NT)   MORDEN

Morden Hall Park (National Trust), Morden Hall Road,
Morden, SM4 5JD   **t:** (020) 8545 6850
w: nationaltrust.org.uk

open: Daily 0800-1800.

description: A green oasis in the heart of South West London. A former deer park with a network of waterways including meadow, wetland and woodland habitats. Spectacular rose garden.

facilities: 💻 🧍 ⛱ ♿

Ham House

Ham House, Ham Street, Ham, Richmond, TW10 7RS
t: (020) 8940 1950   **w:** nationaltrust.org.uk

open:	House: Apr-Oct, Mon-Wed, Sat-Sun 1300-1700. Garden: All year, Mon-Wed, Sat-Sun 1100-1800.
admission:	£9.00
description:	The most complete survivor of 17thC fashion and power. Built in 1610 and enlarged in the 1670s, it was at the heart of Restoration court life and intrigue. Significant formal garden.
facilities:	� ✗ ⊼ ♿

Kew Gardens
(Royal Botanic Gardens)

Kew Gardens (Royal Botanic Gardens),
Kew, Richmond, TW9 3AB
t: (020) 8332 5655   **w:** kew.org

open:	Apr-Aug, daily 0930-1830. Sep-Oct, daily 0930-1800. Nov-Jan, daily 0930-1615. Feb-Mar, daily 0930-1730.
admission:	£12.25
description:	A World Heritage Site with stunning vistas, magnificent glasshouses and beautiful landscapes beside the River Thames. It represents nearly 250 years of historical gardens, and is home to over 30,000 types of plant.
facilities:	▬ ✗ ⊼ ♿

Hampton Court Palace

SURREY

Hampton Court Palace, Surrey, KT8 9AU
t: 0870 752 7777   **w:** hrp.org.uk

open:	Apr-Oct, daily 1000-1800. Nov-Mar, daily 1000-1630.
admission:	£12.30
description:	Explore Henry VIII's state apartments, where history is brought to life with costumed guides. See the historic royal gardens and the world-famous maze - the oldest-surviving hedge maze still in use.
facilities:	♿ 👟 ⛩ ♿

National Wildflower Centre

KNOWSLEY

National Wildflower Centre, Court Hey Park,
Knowsley, L16 3NA   **t:** (0151) 738 1913   **w:** nwc.org.uk

open:	1 Mar-1 Sep 1000-1700, last entry 1600.
admission:	£3.00
description:	A peaceful haven in an otherwise busy world. Full events programme, including Wildflower Heroes events and workshops - all ages and abilities welcome. Pre-booked groups welcome. Seasonal wildflower displays, children's play area (visitor centre charge ap
facilities:	♿ 👟 ⛩ ♿

LIVERPOOL

Croxteth Hall and Country Park

Croxteth Hall and Country Park, Croxteth Hall Lane, Muirhead Avenue, Liverpool, L12 0HB
t: (0151) 228 5311   **w:** croxteth.co.uk

open: See website for details.

description: An Edwardian stately home set in 500 acres of countryside (woodlands and pasture), featuring a Victorian walled garden and animal collection.

facilities:

LIVERPOOL

Speke Hall, Gardens and Woodland (NT)

Speke Hall, Gardens and Woodland (National Trust), The Walk, Liverpool, L24 1XD   **t:** (0151) 427 7231
w: nationaltrust.org.uk

open: See website for details.
admission: £6.50

description: A wonderful, rambling Tudor mansion with rich Victorian interiors, set in a wooded estate on the banks of the Mersey with views of Wirral and North Wales.

facilities:

Peter Beales Roses

Peter Beales Roses, London Road, Attleborough, NR17 1AY
t: (01953) 454707

open:	All year, Mon-Sat 0900-1700, Sun, Bank Hols 1000-1600.
description:	Two and a half acres of display rose garden set in rural surroundings.
facilities:	♿ 🍴 🥾 🪑 ♿

East Ruston Old Vicarage Garden

East Ruston Old Vicarage Garden, East Ruston Old Vicarage, East Ruston, NR12 9HN   **t:** (01692) 650432
w: e-ruston-oldvicaragegardens.co.uk

open:	Apr-Oct, Wed, Fri, Sat-Sun, Bank Hols 1400-1730.
admission:	£5.00
description:	A 20-acre exotic garden separated into sections including the Tropical Borders, Mediterranean Garden, Sunken Garden, Autumn Borders, Kitchen Garden and Wildflower Meadows.
facilities:	🥾 🪑 ♿

Gooderstone Water Gardens

Gooderstone Water Gardens, The Street, Gooderstone,
PE33 9BP   **t:** (01603) 712913
w: gooderstonewatergardens.co.uk

open: Daily 1000-1800.
admission: £4.00

description: Water gardens covering 6.5
acres, with trout stream, four ponds,
waterways, mature trees, colourful plants,
nature trails, 13 bridges. Tearoom with
home-made cakes and disabled toilets.

facilities:

Congham Hall Herb Garden

Congham Hall Herb Garden, Lynn Road, Grimston, PE32 1AH
t: (01485) 600250

open: Apr-Oct, daily 1400-1600.

description: Garden with over 650 varieties of herbs in
formal beds with wild flowers and a potager
garden. Over 250 varieties of herbs for sale in
pots.

facilities:

Norfolk Lavender Limited

Norfolk Lavender Limited, Caley Mill, Heacham,
PE31 7JE   **t:** (01485) 570384   **w:** norfolk-lavender.co.uk

open: Apr-Oct, daily 0900-1700.
                   Nov-Mar, daily 0900-1600.

description: Lavender is distilled from
                   the flowers and the oil
                   made into a wide range of gifts. There is a
                   slide show when the distillery is not working.

facilities: ☕ 🐕 ♿

Mannington Gardens and Countryside

Mannington Gardens and Countryside, Mannington Hall,
Norwich, NR11 7BB   **t:** (01263) 584175
w: manningtongardens.co.uk

open: Gardens: May, Sep, Sun 1200-1700. Jun-Aug,
                   Wed-Fri 1100-1700. Countryside: Daily.
admission: £4.00

description: Gardens with a lake, moat, woodland and
                   an outstanding rose collection. There is
                   also a Saxon church with Victorian follies,
                   countryside walks and trails with guide
                   booklets.

facilities: ☕ 🏃 🏓 ♿

Plantation Garden

The Plantation Garden, 4 Earlham Road, Norwich, NR2 3DB
t: (01603) 624256   w: plantationgarden.co.uk

open:	Daily 0900-1800.
admission:	£2.00

description:	A rare surviving example of a private Victorian town garden, created between 1856-1897 in a former medieval chalk quarry and undergoing restoration by volunteers.

facilities:	⚔ ⊼ ♿

Raveningham Gardens

Raveningham Gardens, The Stables, Raveningham,
NR14 6NS   t: (01508) 548152   w: raveningham.com

open:	Apr-Aug, Mon-Fri 1100-1600, Bank Hols 1400-1700.
admission:	£4.00

description:	Extensive gardens surrounding an elegant Georgian house provide the setting for many rare, variegated and unusual plants and shrubs, with sculptures, parkland and a church.

facilities:	🐕 ♿ᴾ

Fairhaven Woodland and Water Garden

SOUTH WALSHAM

Fairhaven Woodland and Water Garden, School Road, South Walsham, NR13 6DZ   **t:** (01603) 270449
w: fairhavengarden.co.uk

open:	May-Aug, daily 1000-1700. Sep-Apr, daily 1000-1600.
admission:	£4.50

description: Delightful natural woodland and water garden with private broad and a 950-year-old oak tree. Spring flowers, candelabra primulas, azaleas and rhododendrons.

facilities: ⬛ 🐕 ♿

Ecotech Centre

SWAFFHAM

Ecotech Centre, Turbine Way, Swaffham, PE37 7HT
t: (01760) 726100   **w:** ecotech.org.uk

open: Mon-Fri 1000-1600 (excl Bank Holidays). May-Sep, open on last Sunday in the month.

description: Environmental visitor attraction, with an organic garden/heritage seed orchard, cafe and shop. We have an Ecotricity E66 climbable wind turbine situated in our grounds (subject to health and safety rules, charges apply and booking is recommended, please p

facilities: ☕ 🦮 ⛱ ♿

Eau Brink Cacti

TILNEY ALL SAINTS

Eau Brink Cacti, Eau Brink Road, Tilney All Saints, PE34 4SQ
t: (01553) 617635

open: Mar-Oct, Mon-Thu, Sun 1000-1700. Nov-Feb, please phone for details.

description: Half an acre of greenhouses housing owner's collection of approximately 1000 mature cacti and succulents grown by the owner from seed over the last 40 years.

facilities:

Walpole Water Gardens

WALPOLE ST PETER

Walpole Water Gardens, Chalk Road, Walpole St Peter, PE14 7PH **t:** 07718 745935 **w:** walpolewatergardens.co.uk

open: Apr-Oct, daily 1000-1900. Nov-Mar, daily 1000-2100.

description: Dominated by water and rocks, with sub-tropical atmosphere, 0.75 acres. Eucalyptus, rockeries and palms. Koi carp, black swans, ducks and peacocks.

facilities:

See pages 2-3 for key to symbols

West Acre Gardens

West Acre Gardens, King's Lynn, West Acre, PE32 1UJ
t: (01760) 755562   **w:** west-norfolk.gov.uk

open:	Feb-Nov, daily 1000-1700.
description:	D-shaped walled garden with extensive display beds with year-round interest and beauty.
facilities:	⚒ ♿

Hoveton Hall Gardens

Hoveton Hall Gardens, Hoveton Hall, Wroxham, NR12 8RJ
t: (01603) 782798   **w:** hovetonhallgardens.co.uk

open:	Apr, Sun, Bank Hols 1030-1700. May-Aug, Wed-Fri, Sun, Bank Hols 1030-1700. Aug, Sun, Bank Hols 1030-1700.
admission:	£4.50
description:	Approximately 15 acres of gardens in a woodland setting with a large walled herbaceous garden and a Victorian kitchen garden. There are also woodland and lakeside walks.
facilities:	⬛ ⚒ ⛩ ♿

Constable Burton Hall Gardens

CONSTABLE BURTON

Constable Burton Hall Gardens, Constable Burton, DL8 5LJ
t: (01677) 450428   **w:** constableburtongardens.co.uk

open:	Apr-Oct, daily 0900-1800.
admission:	£3.00

description: A terraced woodland garden attached to a beautiful Palladian house (not open) designed by John Carr. Near the main entrance drive is a stream, bog garden and rockery.

facilities: 🐕 🏕 ♿

Paddock Farm Water Gardens

DALTON-ON-TEES

Paddock Farm Water Gardens, West Lane, Dalton-on-Tees, DL2 2PT   **t:** (01325) 378286   **w:** paddock-farm.co.uk

open: Apr-Oct, Mon-Sat 1000-1800, Sun 1100-1700.
Mov-Mar, Tue-Sat 1000-1800, Sun 1100-1700.

description: Nine unique, individually designed gardens, taking inspiration from the Mediterranean to the Orient. Bridge, waterfall, pond and pagoda. Garden centre with experienced, friendly staff. Tearoom overlooking the gardens.

facilities: 🍴 🏕 ♿

RHS Garden Harlow Carr

RHS Garden Harlow Carr, Crag Lane, (off B6162 Otley Road), Harrogate, HG3 1QB   **t:** (01423) 565418
w: rhs.org.uk

open:	Mar-Oct, daily 0930-1800. Nov-Feb, daily 0930-1600.
admission:	£6.00

description: Spectacular 58 acres offering interest for all seasons - from vegetables to wildflowers and alpines to woodland. Bettys Cafe tea rooms and shop offering delicious food and drinks.

facilities:

Helmsley Walled Garden

Helmsley Walled Garden, Cleveland Way, Helmsley, YO62 5AH   **t:** (01439) 771427
w: helmsleywalledgarden.co.uk

open:	Apr-Oct, daily 1030-1700.
admission:	£4.00

description: A five-acre walled garden within the grounds of Duncombe Park. Constructed in 1756, the garden was derelict for many years but is now being restored by staff and volunteers.

facilities:

Walled Garden at Scampston

The Walled Garden at Scampston, Scampston Hall, Malton, YO17 8NG   **t:** (01944) 758224   **w:** scampston.co.uk

open:	Apr-Oct, daily 1000-1700.
admission:	£5.00
description:	An inspired contemporary garden designed by the internationally acclaimed Piet Oudolf, winner of Gold and Best in Show at Chelsea in 2000. Rare plants for sale, restaurant.
facilities:	

Forbidden Corner

The Forbidden Corner, Tupgill Park Estate, Coverham, Middleham, DL8 4TJ   **t:** (01969) 640638
w: yorkshirenet.co.uk/theforbiddencorner

open:	Apr-Oct, Mon-Sat 1200-1800, Sun, Bank Hols 1000-1800.
admission:	£8.00
description:	A unique labyrinth of tunnels, chambers, follies and surprises created in a four-acre garden in the heart of the Yorkshire Dales to challenge and delight children of all ages.
facilities:	

Green Garden Herbs

Green Garden Herbs, 13 West Bank,
Carlton, Nr Selby, DN14 9PZ
t: (01405) 860708
w: greengardenherbs.co.uk

open: Mar-Sep, Mon, Wed-Sun, 1000-
1700.

description: Small, independent herb nursery, specialising
in aromatic, culinary, medicinal and
ornamental herb plants. Lavender a speciality.
Groups welcome, especially coach trips.

facilities: 🍴 🛝 ♿

Rievaulx Terrace & Temples (NT)

Rievaulx Terrace & Temples (National Trust),
The National Trust, Rievaulx, YO62 5LJ
t: (01439) 798340   **w:** nationaltrust.org.uk

open: Apr-Sep, daily 1100-1800. Oct, daily 1100-
1700.
admission: £4.00

description: An 18thC grass-covered terrace, landscaped
from wooded hillside with views of Rievaulx
Abbey. Two classical temples, one furnished
and decorated as a dining room. National
Trust shop.

facilities: 🐕 ♿

Fountains Abbey and Studley Royal

RIPON

Fountains Abbey and Studley Royal Water Garden, Ripon, HG4 3DY **t:** (01765) 608888 **w:** fountainsabbey.org.uk

open: Mar-Oct, daily 1000-1700. Nov-Feb, daily 1000-1600.
admission: £6.50

description: The largest monastic ruin in Britain, founded by Cistercian monks in 1132. Landscaped garden laid 1720-1740 with lake, formal water garden, temples and deer park.

facilities:

Newby Hall & Gardens

RIPON

Newby Hall & Gardens, Ripon, HG4 5AE
t: 0845 450 4068 **w:** newbyhall.com

open: House; Apr-Jun, Tue-Sun1200-1700. Jul-Aug, daily 1200-1700. Sep, Tue-Sun 1200-1700. Gardens; Apr-Jun, Tue-Sun 1100-1730. Jul-Aug, daily 1100-1730. Sep, Tue-Sun 1100-1730.
admission: £9.50

description: One of England's renowned Adam houses, an exceptional example of 18thC interior decoration. Contents include unique Gobelins tapestry room, classical statuary and fine Chippendale furniture.

facilities:

See pages 2-3 for key to symbols

Parcevall Hall Gardens

Parcevall Hall Gardens, Parceval Hall, Skyreholme, BD23 6DE
t: (01756) 720311   **w:** parcevallhallgardens.co.uk

open: Apr-Oct, daily 1000-1800.
admission: £5.00

description: The 16 acres of formal and woodland gardens offer magnificent views, and contain many specimen trees and shrubs collected from Western China and the Himalayas.

facilities: 🍵 🐕 🪑

Sutton Park

Sutton Park, Sutton-on-the-Forest, YO61 1DP
t: (01347) 810249   **w:** statelyhome.co.uk

open: Apr-Sep, daily 1100-1700.
admission: £3.50

description: Georgian stately home with fine furniture, magnificent plasterwork by Cortese and paintings from Buckingham House, now Buckingham Palace. Important collection of porcelain. Wonderful award-winning gardens.

facilities: 🍵 🐕 🪑

Yorkshire Lavender

Yorkshire Lavender, Terrington, YO60 6PB
t: (01653) 648008   **w:** lavenderland.co.uk

open:	Apr-Oct, daily 1000-1700.
description:	The North of England's premier lavender attraction/herb nursery is set in a hillside farm of 60 acres within the Howardian Hills, an Area of Outstanding Natural Beauty.
facilities:	☕ 🥢 ♿

Thorp Perrow Arboretum & Falconry Centre

Thorp Perrow Arboretum & Falconry Centre, Thorp
Perrow, DL8 2PR   **t:** (01677) 425323   **w:** thorpperrow.com

open:	Daily, dawn-dusk.
admission:	£5.95
description:	One of the largest collections of trees and shrubs in the North of England, set in 85 acres of woodland. Four national collections: ash, lime, walnut and laburnum.
facilities:	☕ 🐕 🪑 ♿

Wolds Way Lavender

Wolds Way Lavender, Deer Park Farm,
Sandy Lane, Wintringham, YO17 8HW
t: (01944) 758641   **w:** deerparkfarm.com

open: Apr-May, daily 1000-1600. Jun-Aug, daily
                   1000-1700. Sep-Oct, daily 1000-1600.

description: Surrounded by mature woodland, on the edge
                   of the picturesque Yorkshire Wolds, the newly
                   created lavender and herb farm is a wonderful
                   and relaxing place to visit.

facilities:

Beningbrough Hall & Gardens (NT)

Beningbrough Hall & Gardens (National Trust), Beningbrough,
York, YO30 1DD   **t:** (01904) 470666   **w:** nationaltrust.org.uk

open: House: Jun, Mon-Wed, Sat-Sun 1200-1700.
                   Jul-Aug, Mon-Wed, Fri-Sun 1200-1700. Sep-
                   Oct, Mon-Wed, Sat-Sun 1200-1700. Grounds:
                   Mar-June, Sep-Oct, Mon-Wed, Sat-Sun 1100-
                   1730. Jul-Aug, Mon-Wed, Fri-Sun 1100-1730.
                   Nov, Jan-Feb Sat-Sun 1100-1530.

admission: £7.00

description: Handsome Baroque house, built in 1716,
                   housing 100 portraits from the National
                   Portrait Gallery—including a Victorian laundry,
                   potting shed and restored walled garden.

facilities:

YORK

Arboretum at Castle Howard

The Arboretum at Castle Howard, York, YO60 7DA
t: (01653) 648650   **w:** kewatch.co.uk

open:	Mar-Oct, daily 1000-1800. Nov, daily 1000-1600.
admission:	£4.50
description:	The Arboretum Trust, a registered charity, holds an amazing collection of rare trees and shrubs collected as seed worldwide. Gathered from Chile to China, from Afghanistan to Australia, all flourish in this quiet corner of North Yorkshire.
facilities:	

YORK

Yorkshire Museum

Yorkshire Museum, Museum Gardens, York, YO1 7FR
t: (01904) 650321   **w:** yorkmuseumstrust.org.uk

open:	Daily 1000-1700.
admission:	£4.50
description:	The award-winning museum is set in ten acres of botanical gardens and displays some of the finest Roman, Anglo-Saxon, Viking and medieval treasures ever discovered in Britain.
facilities:	

Castle Ashby Gardens

CASTLE ASHBY

Castle Ashby Gardens, Castle Ashby House, Castle Ashby, NN7 1LQ   **t:** (01604) 696187   **w:** castleashby.co.uk

open:	Apr-Sep, daily 1000-1800. Oct-Mar, daily 1000-1630.
admission:	£2.80

description: An Elizabethan mansion with Capability Brown gardens and an arboretum containing some superb mature trees. The gardens are renowned for their native wild flowers and a wide range of flowering bulbs.

facilities: 🍴 ⛱ ♿

Cottesbrooke Hall and Gardens

COTTESBROOKE

Cottesbrooke Hall and Gardens, Cottesbrooke, NN6 8PF
t: (01604) 505808   **w:** cottesbrookehall.co.uk

open:	May-Jun, Wed-Thu 1400-1730. Jul-Sep, Thu, Bank Hols 1400-1730.
admission:	£7.50

description: A magnificent Queen Anne house dating from 1702, set in delightful rural Northamptonshire. It is reputed to be the pattern for Jane Austen's Mansfield Park.

facilities: ☕ 🍴 ♿

Deene Park

DEENE

Deene Park, Deene, NN17 3EW
t: (01780) 450223 **w:** deenepark.com

open: Apr-May, Bank Hols 1100-1600. Jun-Aug, Sun 1400-1700.

admission: £6.50

description: Acquired by the Brudenell family in 1514 and lived in by their descendants including the 7th Earl of Cardigan (Charge of the Light Brigade). Gardens, teas and gift shop.

facilities:

Haddonstone Show Gardens

EAST HADDON

Haddonstone Show Gardens, The Forge House, Church Lane, East Haddon, NN6 8DB
t: (01604) 770711 **w:** haddonstone.com

open: All year, Mon-Fri 0900-1700.

description: See Haddonstone's classic garden ornaments in the beautiful setting of the walled manor gardens - planters, statuary, fountains and even follies.

facilities:

Kelmarsh Hall and Gardens

Kelmarsh Hall and Gardens, Estate Office, Kelmarsh Hall, Kelmarsh, NN6 9LY **t:** (01604) 686543 **w:** kelmarsh.com

open:	House: Apr-Sep, Thu, Bank Hols 1400-1700. Gardens: Apr-Sep, Tue-Thu, Sun, Bank Hols 1400-1700.
admission:	£5.00
description:	Built 1732 to a James Gibbs design, Kelmarsh Hall is surrounded by its working estate, grazed parkland and beautiful gardens. Successive owners and influences have left their imprint on the Palladian house and gardens.
facilities:	

Coton Lodge

Coton Lodge, West Haddon Road, Guilsborough, Northampton, NN6 8QE **t:** (01604) 740215
w: cottonlodge.co.uk

open:	May-Sep, Thu-Fri, Sun 1200-1700.
admission:	£3.50
description:	Mature two-acre garden with panoramic views over beautiful, unspoilt countryside. Intimate enclosed areas are complemented by an informal woodland stream and pond, giving interest throughout the seasons.
facilities:	

Coton Manor Gardens

Coton Manor Gardens, Nr Guilsborough, Northampton,
NN6 8RQ   **t:** (01604) 740219   **w:** cotonmanor.co.uk

open:	Apr-Sep, Tue-Sat , Bank Hols 1200-1730. Apr-May, Sun 1200-1730.
admission:	£5.00
description:	A ten-acre garden lying in the peaceful Northamptonshire countryside. Originally laid out in the 1920s by the grandparents of the current owner, it comprises a number of smaller gardens.
facilities:	

Stoke Park Pavilions

Stoke Park Pavilions, Stoke Bruerne, NN12 7RZ
t: (01604) 862329

open:	Aug, daily 1300-1800.
admission:	£3.00
description:	Two 17thC pavilions and a colonnade attributed to Inigo Jones and restored in 1954. Extensive gardens.
facilities:	

Howick Hall Gardens

ALNWICK

Howick Hall Gardens, Estate Office, Howick Hall, Alnwick, NE66 3LB **t:** (01665) 577285 **w:** howickhallgardens.org.uk

open: Apr-Oct, daily 1200-1800. Nov-Mar, Sat-Sun 1200-1600.

admission: £4.50

 **description:** Lovely flower, shrub and rhododendron gardens. Extensive grounds with a collection of shrubs in woodland garden, formal gardens around the house, a bog garden and new arboretum (2006).

facilities: ▆ 🕱 ⏃ ♿

Hulne Park

ALNWICK

Hulne Park, c/o Estate Office, Alnwick Castle, Alnwick, NE66 1NQ **t:** (01665) 510777 **w:** alnwickcastle.com

open: All year, Mon-Sun, Bank Hols 1100-1800.

description: Parkland, Gothic tower, lovely views and good walking. No dogs, cycles or vehicles are allowed in the park.

facilities: 🕱

Alnwick Garden

The Alnwick Garden, Denwick Lane, Alnwick, NE66 1YU
t: (01665) 511350   w: alnwickgarden.com

open:	Apr-May, daily 1000-1800. Jun-Sep,daily, 1000-1900. Oct, daily 1000-1800. Nov-Mar, daily 1000-1600.
admission:	£8.00
description:	An exciting, contemporary garden with beautiful and unique gardens, features and structures, brought to life with water. Fantastic eating, drinking and shopping. Events throughout the year.
facilities:	▭ 🐾 ⛩ ♿

Belsay Hall, Castle and Gardens

Belsay Hall, Castle and Gardens, Belsay, NE20 0DX
t: (01661) 881636
w: english-heritage.org.uk

open:	See website for details.
admission:	£5.50
description:	Home of the Middleton family for 600 years. Thirty acres of landscaped gardens and winter garden. Fourteenth-century castle, ruined 17thC manor house and neoclassical hall.
facilities:	▭ 🐾 ⛩ ♿

Ford Nursery

BERWICK-UPON-TWEED

Ford Nursery, Berwick-upon-Tweed, TD15 2PZ
t: (01890) 820379   w: fordnursery.co.uk

open:	Mar-Sep, daily 1000-1700. Oct-Jan, daily 1000-1600.
description:	Garden nursery situated in the grounds of a walled garden. Container-grown shrubs, perennials, alpines, ground-cover plants, trees, grasses and demonstration gardens.
facilities:	⚒ ♿

Herterton House Garden Nursery

CAMBO

Herterton House Garden Nursery, Hartington, Cambo,
NE61 4BN   t: (01670) 774278

open: Apr-Sep, Mon, Wed, Fri-Sun,
Bank Hols 1330-1730.
admission: £3.00

description:	One acre of formal gardens inside stone walls around a 16thC farmhouse incorporating topiary, physic, flower and nursery gardens, and fancy garden with gazebo.
facilities:	⚒

Chipchase Castle

Chipchase Castle, Wark, Chillingham, NE48 3NT
t: (01434) 230203

open:	Jun, daily 1400-1700.
admission:	£5.00

description: One of the best examples of Jacobean architecture in the Borders. Chapel, 14thC pele tower, walled vegetable garden, wild garden with lake, nursery garden selling plants.

facilities: ♨ 🐕 ♿

Dilston Physic Garden Ltd

Dilston Physic Garden, Dilston Mill House, Corbridge, NE45 5QZ   **t:** (01434) 673593   **w:** dilstonphysicgarden.com

open:	Apr-Sep, Wed-Thu 1100-1600.
admission:	£4.00

description: An unusual and inspiring garden containing over 500 species of medicinal plants, and a wonderful place in which to relax and learn about the healing power of medicinal herbs.

facilities: ✗

Chesters Walled Garden

Chesters Walled Garden, The Chesters, Humshaugh,
Hexham, NE46 4BQ   **t:** (01434) 681483
w: chesterswalledgarden.co.uk

open:	Apr-Oct, daily 1000-1700.
admission:	£2.50

description: Beautiful two-acre walled garden containing a unique extensive herb collection, Roman garden, National Collection of thyme, large herbaceous borders, herbal gift shop and nursery.

facilities:

Garden Station

The Garden Station, Langley, Hexham, NE47 5LA
t: (01434) 684391   **w:** thegardenstation.co.uk

open:	May-Aug, Tue-Sun, Bank Hols 1000-1700.
description:	An attractive, restored Victorian railway station in a woodland garden. A unique, tranquil place with gardening and art courses, woodland walk, unusual plants and refreshments.

facilities:

Longframlington Gardens

Longframlington Gardens, Swarland Road, Longframlington,
NE65 8BE   **t:** (01665) 570382
w: longframlingtongardens.co.uk

open:	Daily 0830-1700.
admission:	£3.95

description: Twelve acres of garden and arboretum walks including a wild-flower meadow, rope art, garden design and nursery and plant centre, all in a peaceful countryside setting with fabulous views.

facilities:

Bide-a-Wee Cottage Gardens and Nursery

Bide-a-Wee Cottage Gardens and Nursery,
Stanton, Morpeth, NE65 8PR
t: (01670) 772262   **w:** bideawee.co.uk

open:	May-Aug, Wed, Sat 1330-1700.
admission:	£2.50

description: Set within the picturesque Northumbrian countryside, a unique garden created from a sandstone quarry, planted with unusual perennials, many available from the nursery.

facilities:

Cragside House, Gardens and Estate

Cragside House, Gardens and Estate,
Cragside, Rothbury, Morpeth,
NE65 7PX   **t:** (01669) 620333
w: nationaltrust.org.uk

open:	House: Apr-Sep, Tue-Sun 1300-1730. Oct, Tue-Sun 1300-1630. Gardens: Apr-Oct, Tue-Sun 1030-1730. Nov, Wed-Sun 1100-1600.
admission:	£11.55
description:	The creation of Lord Armstrong, Cragside is a garden of breathtaking drama, whatever the season. This magnificent estate provides one of the last shelters for the endangered red squirrel.
facilities:	🍴 ✕ 🛋 ♿

Wallington House, Walled Garden and Grounds

Wallington House, Walled Garden and Grounds, Wallington,
Cambo, Morpeth, NE61 4AR   **t:** (01670) 773600
w: nationaltrust.org.uk

open: House: Apr-Aug, Mon, Wed-Sun
1300-1730. Sep-Oct, Mon, Wed-Sun
1300-1630. Walled Garden: Apr-Sep,
daily 1000-1900. Oct, daily 1000-1800.
Nov-Feb, daily 1000-1600. Grounds:
Daily, dawn-dusk.

admission:	£8.80
description:	The country home of the Trevelyan family sits in 100 acres of lawns, lakes and woodland. Visit its beautiful walled garden.
facilities:	🍴 🐕 🛋 ♿

Kirkley Hall Gardens

PONTELAND

Kirkley Hall Gardens, Kirkley Hall, Ponteland, NE20 0AQ
t: (01670) 841200   **w:** northland.ac.uk

open: All year, Mon-Fri 0830-1700.

description: Ornamental gardens and grounds with all
                  plants labelled. Shrubs, ornamental borders,
                  sunken garden and alpines. Wall-trained fruit
                  trees and greenhouse plants.

facilities:

Seaton Delaval Hall

WHITLEY BAY

Seaton Delaval Hall, Seaton Sluice, Whitley Bay, NE26 4QR
t: (0191) 237 1493

open: Jun-Sep, Wed, Sun 1400-1800.
admission: £4.00

description: A splendid English baroque house comprising
                  a centre block between two arcaded and
                  pedimented wings. The east wing contains
                  fine stables, and there are gardens with
                  statues.

facilities:

Naturescape Wildflower Farm

Naturescape Wildflower Farm, Coach Gap Lane, Off Harby Road, Langar, NG13 9HP **t:** (01949) 860592
w: naturescape.co.uk

open: Apr-Sep, daily 1130-1700.

description: Range of wild flowers in bloom over 30 acres of fields which attract associated butterflies, birds and mammals, and a wildlife garden featuring many habitats.

facilities: ▣ 🐕 ♿

Meditation Centre and Japanese Garden

Meditation Centre and Japanese Garden, Pureland, North Clifton, NG23 7AT **t:** (01777) 228567

open: Meditation centre: All year, Tue-Fri 1030-1730, Sat-Sun 1000-1730. Japanese Garden: Mar-Jul, Oct, Tue-Fri 1030-1730, Sat-Sun 1000-1730. Aug-Sep, Tue-Fri 1030-1730, Sat-Sun 1000-1730, 1900-2200.

admission: £5.00

description: A traditional Japanese garden open to the public.

facilities: ▣ 🍴 ♿

Teversal Manor Gardens

Teversal Manor Gardens, Buttery Lane, Teversal Old Village, Teversal, NG17 3JN   **t:** (01623) 554569

open:	Apr-Dec, Thu-Sat 1000-1730, Sun, Bank Hols 1100-1700.
admission:	£4.50

description:	A handsome 18th century manor house set in the small unspoilt village of Old Teversal.
facilities:	⬛ ⚔ ♿

Felley Priory Garden

Felley Priory Garden, Underwood, NG16 5FL
t: (01773) 810230

open:	All year, Tue, Wed, Fri 0900-1300.
admission:	£3.00
description:	A plantman's garden full of unusual and old-fashioned perennials, shrubs and trees.
facilities:	⬛ ⚔ ♿

Capel Manor College & Gardens

Capel Manor College & Gardens, Bullsmoor Lane, Enfield, EN1 4RQ   **t:** 0845 612 2122   **w:** capel.ac.uk

open: Mar-Oct 1000-1800, last entry 1630. Nov-Feb, weekdays 1000-1730, last entry 1600.

admission: £4.00

description: Thirty acres of beautiful themed gardens including a Japanese Garden, Italianate Maze, Gardening Which? Trial Gardens and Kim Wilde's Jungle Gym Garden, plus our animal corner, await you. Shows and events throughout the year, from the spectacular Spring G

facilities:

Buscot Park

Buscot Park, Buscot, SN7 8BU
t: (01367) 240786   **w:** buscot-park.com

open: Apr-Sep, see website for details.
admission: £7.00

description: An 18thC Palladian-style house with park and water garden. Home of the Faringdon collection of paintings and furniture. The park is landscaped with extensive water gardens.

facilities:

Harcourt Arboretum

NUNEHAM COURTENAY

Harcourt Arboretum, Nuneham Courtenay, OX44 9PX
t: (01865) 343501   **w:** botanic-garden.ox.ac.uk

open:	Apr, Sep-Oct, Mar, daily 0900-1700. May-Aug, daily 0900-1800. Jan-Feb, Nov-Dec, daily 0900-1730.
admission:	£2.70
description:	Eighty acres of trees, shrubs, woodland, meadow and pond. Many trees over 200 years old. Highlights include Japanese Acers, a bluebell woodland and wild-flower meadows.
facilities:	🏃 ♿

University of Oxford Botanic Garden

OXFORD

University of Oxford Botanic Garden, Rose Lane, Oxford, OX1 4AZ   **t:** (01865) 286690
w: botanic-garden.ox.ac.uk

open:	Apr-Nov, daily 1000-1700. Dec-Mar, Mon-Fri 1000-1630.
description:	Over 6,000 species of plants in garden, glasshouses, rock and water gardens, housed within the oldest botanic garden in Britain.
facilities:	🏃 ♿

Waterperry Gardens Limited

Waterperry Gardens Limited,
Waterperry, OX33 1JZ
t: (01844) 339254
w: waterperrygardens.co.uk

open:	Apr-Oct, daily 0900-1730. Nov-Feb, daily 1000-1700.
admission:	£4.50
description:	Ornamental gardens covering six acres of the 83-acre 18thC Waterperry House estate. A Saxon village church, garden shop teashop, art and craft gallery are found within the grounds.
facilities:	

Blenheim Palace

Blenheim Palace, Woodstock, OX20 1PX
t: (01993) 811091   **w:** blenheimpalace.com

open: Palace and Gardens: Feb-Oct, daily 1030-1730. Nov-9 Dec, Wed-Sun 1030-1730. Park: All year, daily 0900-1645.
admission: £16.00

description:	World Heritage site set in 2,100 acres of parkland landscaped by Capability Brown. Home to 11th Duke of Marlborough and the birthplace of Winston Churchill. Interiors feature superb carving, hand-painted ceilings and renowned collections.
facilities:	

Barnsdale Gardens

Barnsdale Gardens, The Avenue, Exton, LE15 8AH
t: (01572) 813200   **w:** barnsdalegardens.co.uk

open:	Apr-May, daily 0900-1700. Jun-Aug, daily 0900-1900. Sep-Oct, daily 0900-1700. Nov-Feb, daily 1000-1600.
admission:	£6.00
description:	Geoff Hamilton's Barnsdale TV Garden, familiar to BBC2 'Gardeners' World' viewers, consists of 37 individual gardens and features, all blending into an eight-acre garden. Small, specialist nursery, licensed coffee shop.
facilities:	

Goldstone Hall Gardens

Goldstone Hall Gardens, Goldstone, TF9 2NA
t: (01630) 661202   **w:** goldstonehall.com

open:	Daily.
description:	Walled garden with acacia, an incomparable stand of hornbeams, natural green beech and views of Staffordshire.
facilities:	

Angel Gardens

Angel Gardens, Springfield, Angel Lane, Ludlow, SY8 3HZ
t: (01584) 890381   **w:** stmem.com/angelgardens

open:	Apr-Oct, Mon, 1200-1700, Sat, 1400-1700, Sun, Bank Hols 1200-1700.
admission:	£4.00

description: Angel Gardens are beautiful ornamental gardens located in an Area of Outstanding Natural Beauty near Ludlow.

facilities: ☕ 🍴 ♿

Wollerton Old Hall Garden

Wollerton Old Hall Garden, Wollerton, Market Drayton, TF9 3NA
t: (01630) 685760
w: wollertonoldhallgarden.com

open:	Apr-Sep, Fri, Sun, Bank Hols 1200-1700.
admission:	£4.80
description:	An example of horticultural excellence, set in the Shropshire countryside. This formal garden, created on a centuries-old site, comprises individual garden rooms, each with its own dazzling display of perennials.
facilities:	☕ 🍴 ♿

Burford House Gardens

TENBURY WELLS

Burford House Gardens, Burford Garden Company, Tenbury Wells, WR15 8HQ **t:** (01584) 810777
w: burford.co.uk

open:	Apr-Dec, Mon-Sun 0900-dusk. Jan-Mar, Mon-Sun 0900-dusk.
admission:	£3.95
description:	Seven acres of beautiful riverside gardens containing the National Clematis Collection. Garden centre bursting with interesting gifts for home and garden.
facilities:	🍵 🐕 🪑 ♿

David Austin Roses

WOLVERHAMPON

David Austin Roses, Bowling Green Lane, Albrighton, Wolverhampon, WV7 3HB **t:** (01902) 376334
w: davidaustinroses.co.uk

open:	Daily 0900-1700.
description:	World-famous rose garden containing over 700 roses of all types, including the Renaissance Garden which is devoted entirely to English roses.
facilities:	🍵 🐕 🪑 ♿

Barrington Court

Barrington Court, Barrington, TA19 0NQ
t: (01460) 241938   **w:** nationaltrust.org.uk

open:	Apr-Sep, Mon-Tue, Thu-Sun 1100-1700. Oct, Mon-Tue, Thu-Sun 1100-1630. Dec, Sat-Sun 1100-1600.
admission:	£7.00

description: Series of beautiful gardens influenced by Gertrude Jekyll including a large kitchen garden designed to support the house.

facilities: 💻 🏃 ⛩ ♿

Botanical Gardens

Botanical Gardens, Royal Victoria Park, Bath, BA1 2XT
t: (01225) 477101
w: visitbath.co.uk

open: All year, daily.

description: Garden contains over 5,000 different varieties of plants from all over the world; one of the finest collections of plants on limestone in the country. Rock garden and pond.

facilities: 💻 🏃 ⛩ ♿

Henrietta Park and
King George V Memorial Garden

Henrietta Park and King George V Memorial Garden,
Henrietta Street, Bath, BA2 6LR   **t:** (01225) 396386
w: visitbath.co.uk

open:	All year, daily.
description:	A seven-acre park close to the city centre, laid out and opened to celebrate the Diamond Jubilee of Queen Victoria in 1897. It includes a garden with many scented plants.
facilities:	🐕 ♿

Cannington College
Heritage Gardens

Cannington College Heritage Gardens, Bridgewater College,
Cannington Centre, Cannington, TA5 2LS
t: (01278) 455464   **w:** cannington.ac.uk

open:	All year, Mon-Fri 0900-1600.
admission:	£2.50
description:	Cannington College gardens have been established for over 75 years and house extensive and rare plant collections.
facilities:	☕ 🐕 ♿

Hestercombe Gardens

Hestercombe Gardens, Cheddon Fitzpaine, TA2 8LG
t: (01823) 413923   **w:** hestercombegardens.com

open:	All year, daily 1000-1800.
admission:	£6.95

description: A unique combination of Georgian landscape, Victorian terrace and Edwardian garden. Walks, streams, temples, vivid colours, formal terraces, woodlands, lakes and cascades.

facilities: 🍽 ⚐ ⛱ ♿

Prior Park Landscape Garden

Prior Park Landscape Garden, Ralph Allen Drive, Combe Down, BA2 5AH   **t:** (01225) 833422   **w:** nationaltrust.org.uk

open:	Apr-Oct, Mon, Wed-Sun 1100-1730. Nov-Feb, Sat-Sun 1100-dusk.
admission:	£4.50

description: Beautiful and intimate 18thC landscaped garden created by Bath entrepreneur Ralph Allen (1693-1764) with advice from the poet Alexander Pope and Capability Brown.

facilities: ⚐ ⛱ ♿

Lower Severalls Garden and Nursery

Lower Severalls Garden and Nursery, Crewkerne, TA18 7NX
t: (01460) 73234   **w:** lowerseveralls.co.uk

open:	Mar-Jul, Tue-Wed, Fri-Sat, Bank Hols 1000-1700. Sep, Tue-Wed, Fri-Sat, 1000-1700.
admission:	£3.00
description:	Enchanting, original garden set in front of 18thC hamstone farmhouse. The informal garden has herbaceous borders and many innovative features with a nursery.
facilities:	🐕 ⛱ ♿

Kelways Plant Centre and Orchid House

Kelways Plant Centre and Orchid House, Barrymore Farm, Picts Hill, Langport, TA10 9EZ   **t:** (01458) 250521
w: kelways.co.uk

open:	All year, Mon-Sat 0900-1700, Sun, Bank Hols 1000-1600.
description:	Plant centre and orchid display house. National collection of peonies open during flowering season in June.
facilities:	🐕 ⛱ ♿

East Lambrook Manor Gardens

SOUTH PETHERTON

East Lambrook Manor Gardens, East Lambrook, South Petherton, TA13 5HH   **t:** (01460) 240328
w: eastlambrook.co.uk

open:	Daily, Bank Hols 1000-1700.
admission:	£3.95
description:	The garden at East Lambrook Manor is recognised throughout the world as the home of English cottage gardening, having been created in the 1940s, 50s and 60s by the late gardening icon, Margery Fish.
facilities:	

Tintinhull Garden

TINTINHULL

Tintinhull Garden, Farm Street, Tintinhull, BA22 8PZ
t: (01935) 822545   **w:** nationaltrust.org.uk

open:	Apr-Oct, Wed-Sun 1100-1700.
admission:	£5.00
description:	A 20thC formal garden surrounding a 17thC house. The layout is divided into areas by walls and hedges, has border colour and plant themes, shrub roses, clematis and kitchen garden.
facilities:	

Time-Trail of Roses

WELLS

The Time-Trail of Roses & Bulbs, Westfield Road, Wells,
BA5 2RB   **t:** (01749) 674677

open: Feb-Jul, 2nd & 4th Sun of each month.
admission: £3.50

description: Rose garden with over 1,000 varieties of rose,
bulbs and snowdrops, planted in chronological
order of their introduction into gardening. Also
a medieval herb garden, trees, shrubs and
perennials.

facilities: ⚒ 🏕

Brodsworth Hall
and Gardens

BRODSWORTH

Brodsworth Hall and Gardens, Brodsworth Hall,
Brodsworth, DN5 7XJ   **t:** (01904) 601974
w: english-heritage.org.uk

open: See website for details.
admission: £6.60

description: One of the most complete surviving examples
of an English Victorian country house
set in 15 acres of formal and informal
gardens and woodland.

facilities: ⊒ ⚒ 🏕 ♿

Cannon Hall Country Park

CAWTHORNE

Cannon Hall Country Park, Cawthorne, S75 4AT
t: (01226) 790270

open: Daily.

description: An 18thC landscaped parkland and formal gardens with lakes. Educational visits, fishing, important collections in the walled garden including extensive and rare pear trees.

facilities: 🍽 🐕 🎪 ♿

Tropical Butterfly House, Wildlifeand Farm

NORTH ANSTON

Tropical Butterfly House, Wildlife and Farm, Hungerhill Farm, Woodsetts Road, North Anston, S25 4EQ
t: (01909) 569416   **w:** butterflyhouse.co.uk

open: Apr-Sep, Mon-Fri 1000-1630, Sat-Sun 1000-1730. Nov-Mar, Mon-Fri 1100-1630, Sat-Sun 1000-1700.

admission: £5.99

description: Exotic butterflies, plants and animals in a natural jungle environment. Falconry Centre, farm animals and pets, Unique Native Fauna and Flora Nature Trail, picnic area, formal gardens, gift shop and cafe.

facilities: 🍽 🎪 ♿

Sheffield Botanical Gardens

Sheffield Botanical Gardens, Clarkehouse Road, Sheffield, S10 2LN   **t:** (0114) 267 6496   **w:** sbg.org.uk

open: Winter: Mon-Fri 0800-1600, Sat-Sun, Bank Hols 1000-1600. Summer: Mon-Fri 0800-dusk, Sat-Sun, Bank Hols 1000-dusk.

description: Extensive gardens with over 5,500 species of plants. The gardens, which are Grade II Listed by English Heritage, were landscaped by Robert Marnock, a famous 19thC landscape designer.

facilities: ☕ 🐕 ♿

Sheffield Winter Gardens

Sheffield Winter Gardens, Surrey Street, Sheffield, S1 2HH **t:** (0114) 273 6681   **w:** sheffield.gov.uk

open: Daily 0800-1800.

description: One of the largest temperate glasshouses to be recently built in the UK, the award-winning Winter Gardens offer a stunning green world in the heart of the city.

facilities: ☕ 🐕 ♿

Wentworth Castle Gardens

STAINBOROUGH

Wentworth Castle Gardens, Lowe Lane, Stainborough, S75 3ET **t:** (01226) 776040 **w:** wentworthcastle.org

open: Apr-Sep, daily 1000-1700. Oct-Mar, daily 1000-1600.

admission: £3.95

description: Wentworth Castle Gardens provide a wonderful day out for all the family. A secret Yorkshire treasure awaits you, hidden away in green rolling hills near Barnsley.

facilities:

National Memorial Arboretum

ALREWAS

National Memorial Arboretum, Croxall Road, Alrewas, DE13 7AR **t:** (01283) 792333
w: nationalmemorialarboretum.org.uk

open: Daily 0900-dusk.

description: A 150-acre arboretum planted as a tribute to the people of the 20th century. Plots include those planted for the Armed and Merchant Services, the police and fire service.

facilities:

Biddulph Grange Garden (National Trust)

BIDDULPH

Biddulph Grange Garden (National Trust), Grange Road, Biddulph, ST8 7SD   **t:** (01782) 517999
w: nationaltrust.org.uk

open:	Apr-Oct, Wed-Sun 1130-1800. Nov, Sat-Sun 1100-1500.
admission:	£6.00
description:	An exciting and rare survival of a high Victorian garden, acquired by the Trust in 1988.

facilities: ☕ 🏃 ⛵ ♿

Trentham Leisure Ltd

TRENTHAM

Trentham Leisure, Stone Road, Trentham, ST4 8AX
t: (01782) 657341   **w:** trenthamleisure.co.uk

open:	Garden: Apr-Sep, daily 1000-1800. Nov-Mar, daily 1000-1600. Woodlands: Daily, dawn-dusk.
admission:	£6.50
description:	Seven-hundred-and-fifty acres of scenic gardens, woodlands and lake, currently undergoing major redevelopment work.

facilities: ☕ 🏃 ⛵ ♿

Weston Park

Weston Park, Weston-under-Lizard, TF11 8LE
t: (01952) 852100   **w:** weston-park.com

open: See website for details.
admission: £4.50

description: The grounds of Weston Park combine 1,000 acres of natural beauty with three centuries of garden design.

facilities: ☕ 🎪 ♿

Chillington Hall

Chillington Hall, Codsall Wood, Wolverhampton, WV8 1RE
t: (01902) 850236   **w:** chillingtonhall.co.uk

open: Jul, Thu, Sun 1400-1700. Aug, Wed-Fri, Sun 1400-1700.
admission: £4.00

description: Georgian house, part-1724 Francis Smith, part-1785 Sir John Soane, fine saloon, grounds and lake by Capability Brown. Extensive woodland walks, lakeside temples and folly.

facilities: 🎪 ⛺ ♿

Walled Garden

The Walled Garden, Park Road, Benhall, IP17 1JB
t: (01728) 602510   **w:** thewalledgarden.co.uk

open:	Apr-Nov, Mar,Tue-Sun 0930-1700. Dec-Feb, Tue-Sat 0930-1700.
description:	A retail nursery and garden selling almost 1,500 varieties of plants, nestling in the warmth of the high wall of an old kitchen garden.
facilities:	⚐ ☂ ♿

East Bergholt Place Garden

East Bergholt Place Garden, East Bergholt Place, East
Bergholt, CO7 6UP   **t:** (01206) 299224

open:	Apr-Sep, daily 1000-1700.
admission:	£3.00
description:	The Place Garden was laid out at the turn of the century and covers 15 acres with fine trees, shrubs, rhododendrons, camellias and magnolias.
facilities:	⚐ ♿

Woottens Plants

Woottens Plants, Blackheath, Wenhaston, Halesworth,
IP19 9HD   **t:** (01502) 478258   **w:** woottensplants.co.uk

open:	Daily 0930-1700.
description:	Plantsman's nursery with huge range of stock. Frequently featured in the press and on television. Unique for the range and quality of its plants.
facilities:	⚔ 🜂 ♿

Helmingham Hall Gardens

Helmingham Hall Gardens, Estate Office, Helmingham,
IP14 6EF   **t:** (01473) 890799   **w:** helmingham.com

open:	May-Sep, Wed, Sun 1400-1800.
admission:	£4.50
description:	Moated and walled garden with many rare roses and possibly the best kitchen garden in Britain. With new rose garden and herb and knot garden created in the early 1980s.
facilities:	▣ 🐕 🜂 ♿

Kentwell Hall and Garden

Kentwell Hall and Garden, Kentwell Hall, Long Melford, CO10 9BA **t:** (01787) 310207 **w:** kentwell.co.uk

open:	See website for details.
admission:	£6.00

description: Moated Tudor mansion, 'a little great house of magical beauty'. Exterior almost unaltered. The present owners have recovered and extended the once noted gardens.

facilities:

Somerleyton Hall and Gardens

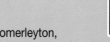

Somerleyton Hall and Gardens, Somerleyton, NR32 5QQ **t:** (01502) 730224 **w:** somerleyton.co.uk

open: Hall: Apr-Jun, Thu, Sun, Bank Hols 1200-1600. Jul-Aug, Tue-Thu, Sun 1200-1600. Sep-Oct, Thu, Sun, Bank Hols 1200-1600. Gardens: Apr-Jun, Thu, Sun, Bank Hols 1000-1700. Jul-Aug, Tue-Thu, Sun 1000-1700. Sep-Oct, Thu, Sun, Bank Hols 1000-1700.

admission: £7.50

description: Early Victorian stately mansion in Anglo-Italian style, with lavish features and fine state rooms. Beautiful 12-acre gardens, with historic yew hedge maze, gift shop.

facilities:

Thornham Walled Garden

The Thornham Walled Garden, Thornham Field Centre Trust,
Red House Yard, Thornham Magna, IP23 8HH
t: (01379) 788700   **w:** thornhamfieldcentre.org

open:	Apr-Oct, Mar, daily 0900-1700. Nov-Feb, daily 0900-1600.
description:	Restored Victorian glasshouses in the idyllic setting of a two-acre walled garden with fruit trees, wide perennial borders, collection of East Anglian geraniums and fern house.
facilities:	

Ramster Gardens

Ramster Gardens, Ramster, Chiddingfold, GU8 4SN
t: (01428) 654167   **w:** ramsterweddings.co.uk

open:	Apr-Jun, daily 1000-1700.
admission:	£5.00
description:	Mature woodland garden of over 20 acres. Flowering shrubs and wild flowers especially good in spring and early summer. Fine trees, magnolias, camellias, azaleas and rhododendrons.
facilities:	

Painshill Park

COBHAM

Painshill Park, Portsmouth Road, Cobham, KT11 1JE
t: (01932) 868113 **w:** painshill.co.uk

open: Mar-Oct 1030-1800, last entry 1630. Nov-Feb 1030-1600 (or dusk), last entry 1500.
admission: £6.60

description: Painshill Park is one of the most important 18thC parks in Europe with 160 acres of authentically restored park, with folly buildings and 18thC plantings. American Roots exhibition (NCCPG award), family events, children's trails, full educational programm

facilities:

Claremont Landscape Garden

ESHER

Claremont Landscape Garden, Portsmouth Road, Esher, KT10 9JG **t:** (01372) 467806 **w:** nationaltrust.org.uk

open: Apr-Oct, daily 1000-1800. Nov-Mar, Tue-Sun 1000-1700.
admission: £5.60

description: One of the earliest-surviving English landscape gardens by Vanbourgh and Bridgeman. Lake, island, view points and avenues with pavilion grotto and turf amphitheatre.

facilities:

See pages 2-3 for key to symbols

Polesden Lacey

Polesden Lacey, Great Bookham, RH5 6BD
t: (01372) 458203   **w:** nationaltrust.org.uk

open:	House: Apr-Oct, Wed-Sun 1100-1700. Gardens: Apr-Oct, daily 1100-1700. Nov-Feb, daily 1100-1600.
admission:	£6.50
description:	A Regency villa, re-modelled after 1906 with collections of paintings, porcelain, tapestries and furniture. Walled rose garden, extensive grounds with landscape walks and woodland.
facilities:	▬ 👭 🗔 ♿

Loseley Park

Loseley Park, Estate Offices, Loseley Park, Guildford,
GU3 1HS   **t:** (01483) 405112   **w:** loseley-park.com

open:	Gardens/grounds: May-Sep, Tue-Sun, Bank Holiday Mon 1100-1700. House: May-Aug, Tue-Thu, Sun, 1300-1700, Bank Holiday Mon 1200-1700.
admission:	£7.00
description:	Steeped in history and home of the More-Molyneux family for nearly 500 years, Loseley House is surrounded by glorious countryside and boasts one of the most beautiful gardens in the country.
facilities:	▬ 👭 🗔 ♿

Winkworth Arboretum

Winkworth Arboretum, The National Trust, Hascombe Road, Hascombe, GU8 4AD   **t:** (01483) 208477
w: nationaltrust.org.uk

open: All year, dawn-dusk.
admission: £5.00

description: One hundred acres of hillside planted with rare trees and shrubs. Good views, lakes, newly-restored boathouse, azaleas, bluebells, wild spring flowers and autumn colours.

facilities:

Gatton Park

Gatton Park, Reigate, RH2 0TW
t: (01737) 649068   **w:** gattonpark.com

open: See website for details.

description: Gatton Park is a spectacular, historic park landscaped by 'Capability' Brown situated at the foot of the North Downs. Enjoy lost gardens, lakes, woodland in stunning setting.

facilities:

Savill Garden,
Windsor Great Park

The Savill Garden, Windsor Great Park, Wick Lane, Englefield
Green, Windsor, TW20 0UU   **t:** (01753) 847518
w: theroyallandscape.co.uk

open:	Apr-Oct, Mar, daily 1000-1800. Nov-Feb, daily 1000-1630.
admission:	£4.00
description:	Woodland garden with adjoining formal rose gardens and herbaceous borders, offering much of great interest and beauty at all seasons. Plant centre, gift shop, restaurant.
facilities:	☕ 🧗 ⛱ ♿

RHS Garden Wisley

RHS Garden Wisley, Wisley, GU23 6QB
t: (01483) 224234   **w:** rhs.org.uk

open:	Apr-Oct, Mar, Mon-Fri 1000-1800, Sat-Sun 0900-1800. Nov-Feb, Mon-Fri 1000-1630, Sat-Sun 0900-1430.
admission:	£7.50
description:	Stretching over 240 acres of glorious garden, Wisley demonstrates the best in British gardening practices, whatever the season. Plant centre, gift shop and restaurant.
facilities:	☕ 🧗 ⛱ ♿

Gisborough Hall

Gisborough Hall, Whitby Lane, Guisborough, TS14 6PT
t: 0870 400 8191   **w:** gisboroughhall.com

open:	All year, Mon-Sat 1000-2300, Sun 1100-2200.
description:	Built in 1857, with the east wing added in 1902, this Grade II Listed Victorian hall has been carefully refurbished and developed as a country-house hotel with landscaped gardens.
facilities:	☕ 🐕 ♿

Nature's World

Nature's World, Ladgate Lane, Acklam, Middlesbrough, TS5 7YN   **t:** (01642) 594895
w: naturesworld.org.uk

open:	Apr-Sep, daily 1000-1700. Oct-Mar, daily 1030-1530.
admission:	£4.00
description:	Demonstration gardens, wildlife pond, white garden, shop, tearoom and unique River Tees model. Futuristic Hydroponicum and Eco Centre now open, powered by renewable energy. Family trails and play areas.
facilities:	☕ 🧗 ⛱ ♿

Saltwell Park

Saltwell Park, Saltwell Road,
Gateshead, NE8 4SF
t: (0191) 433 5900
w: gateshead.gov.uk

open: Daily, dawn-dusk.

description: One of Britain's finest examples of a Victorian Park offering bedding displays, rose garden, play areas, shrubbery, a lake with boating and bowls.

facilities: 🍵 🐕 ⛱ ♿

Birkheads Secret Gardens & Nursery

Birkheads Secret Gardens & Nursery, Birkheads Lane, nr Hedley Hall Woods, Sunniside, Newcastle upon Tyne, NE16 5EL   **t:** (01207) 232262   **w:** birkheadsnursery.co.uk

open: Mar-Oct, Tue-Sun 1000-1700.
admission: £2.50

description: A magical place, along winding paths into hidden, individually themed areas making up the three-acre country garden. Rich with colour, scent, ideas, inspirational plants and wildlife. Before browsing the nursery for unusual plants, enjoy panoramic views and freshly ground coffee on the terrace of the topiary garden.

facilities: 🍵 ✗ ♿

Mowbray Park

Mowbray Park, Burdon Road, Sunderland, SR1 1PP
t: (0191) 553 2323   **w:** sunderland.gov.uk

open: All year, Mon-Sat 1000-1700, Sun 1400-1700.

description: The park recreates the heyday of Victorian leisure with features for young and old alike. Nearby, the Winter Gardens will fascinate and entertain - all for free!

facilities: 🖳 ⚔ ♿

Sunderland Museum and Winter Gardens

Sunderland Museum and Winter Gardens, Burdon Road, Sunderland, SR1 1PP   **t:** (0191) 553 2323
w: twmuseums.org.uk/sunderland

open: All year, Mon-Sat 1000-1700, Sun 1400-1700.

description: Stunning winter gardens, with 1,500 of the world's most exotic flowers, plants and trees. Dramatic 'Museum Street', 11 galleries, tree-top walkway, shop, brasserie and lifts.

facilities: 🖳 ⚔ ♿

Washington Old Hall

Washington Old Hall, The Avenue, Washington Village, Washington, NE38 7LE   **t:** (0191) 416 6879
w: nationaltrust.org.uk

open:	House: Apr-Oct, Mon-Wed, Sun 1100-1700. Gardens: Apr-Oct, Mon-Wed, Sun 1000-1700.
admission:	£4.40

description: A delightful stone-built manor house on the site of the home of the ancestors of George Washington. Displays, gardens and 17thC room recreations. A gem of a property!

facilities: 💺 🏃 🏕 ♿

Upton House

Upton House, Banbury, OX15 6HT
t: (01295) 670266   **w:** nationaltrust.org.uk

open:	Mar-Oct, Mon-Wed, Sat-Sun 1200-1700. Nov, Sat-Sun 1200-1600.
admission:	£8.00

description: A late-17thC house, remodelled from 1927-1929 for the 2nd Viscount Bearsted, containing his internationally important collection of paintings and porcelain. Spectacular garden.

facilities: 💺 🏃 🏕 ♿

Jephson Gardens

Jephson Gardens, Parade, Leamington Spa, CV32 4AB
t: (01926) 456211   **w:** warwickdc.gov.uk

open: Daily 0800-dusk.

description: World-famous prestigious floral displays. Notable and rare specimen trees and shrubs. Lake  and fountain replicas as at Hampton Court. Grade II Listed garden.

facilities: ☕ 🐕 ♿

Dobbies World

Dobbies World, Nuneaton Road, Mancetter, CV9 1RF
t: (01827) 713438   **w:** visitplantasia.co.uk

open: Mar-Oct, Mon-Sat 0930-1800, Sun 0930-1700. Nov-Feb, daily 0930-1600.
admission: £5.75

description: A 30-acre site including Maze World, Plantasia and a deer park with a hide and picnic area. A great day out.

facilities: ☕ 🏃 🪑 ♿

Birmingham Botanical Gardens & Glasshouses

BIRMINGHAM

The Birmingham Botanical Gardens & Glasshouses, Westbourne Road, Edgbaston, Birmingham, B15 3TR
t: (0121) 454 1860   **w:** birminghambotanicalgardens.org.uk

open: Apr-Sep, Mon-Sat 0900-1900, Sun 1000-1900, last entry 1830. Oct-Mar, Mon-Sat 0900-1700, Sun 1000-1700, last entry 1630 (excl 25 Dec).
admission: £6.50

description: Four glasshouses take visitors from tropical rainforest to arid desert conditions with insectivorous plants, giant cacti, tree ferns cycads, orchids and citrus fruits. Outside, 15 acres of landscaped gardens.

facilities: 🍵 🔥 ⛱ ♿

Ryton Organic Gardens

COVENTRY

Ryton Organic Gardens, Wolston Lane, Ryton-on-Dunsmore, Coventry, CV8 3LG   **t:** (024) 7630 3517
w: gardenorganic.org.uk

open: Daily 0900-1700.
admission: £5.00

description: The UK's national centre for organic gardening with ten acres of glorious gardens and the Vegetable Kingdom, an exciting £2 million interactive visitors' centre.

facilities: 🍵 🔥 ♿

Walsall Arboretum

WALSALL

Walsall Arboretum, Lichfield Street, Walsall, WS4 2BU
t: (01922) 653148 **w:** walsallarboretum.co.uk

open: Summer: daily 0700-2130. Winter: daily 0700-1600.

description: A picturesque Victorian park with over 170 acres of gardens, lakes and parkland. Home to the famous Walsall Illuminations each autumn.

facilities:

Wakehurst Place Gardens

ARDINGLY

Wakehurst Place Gardens, Ardingly, RH17 6TN
t: (01444) 894066 **w:** kew.org

open: Mar-Oct, daily 1000-1800. Nov-Feb, daily 1000-1630.

admission: £8.50

description: Extensive estate gardens administered by Royal Botanic Gardens, Kew and has a series of lakes, ponds and an important collection of exotic trees, plants and shrubs.

facilities:

See pages 2-3 for key to symbols

Holly Gate Cactus Nursery and Garden

ASHINGTON

Holly Gate Cactus Nursery and Garden, Billingshurst Road, Ashington, RH20 3BB   **t:** (01903) 892930
w: hollygatecactus.co.uk

open: Daily 0900-1700.
admission: £2.00

description: A famous collection of over 20,000 rare cactus and succulent plants from around the world landscaped in 10,000sq ft of glasshouses.

facilities: ⚅ ⛰ ♿

Standen

EAST GRINSTEAD

Standen, West Hoathly Road, East Grinstead, RH19 4NE
t: (01342) 323029
w: nationaltrust.org.uk

open: Apr-Jul, Wed-Sun 1100-1630. Aug, Mon, Wed-Sun 1100-1630. Sep-Oct, Wed-Sun 1100-1630. Nov-Dec, Mar, Sat-Sun 1100-1500.
admission: £7.50

description: A large family house built in 1894, designed by Philip Webb, which remains unchanged with its Morris textiles and wallpapers. Fine views from the hillside gardens.

facilities: ⊟ ⚅ ⛰ ♿

Denmans Garden

Denmans Garden, Denmans Lane, Fontwell,
BN18 0SU **t:** (01243) 542808
w: denmans-garden.co.uk

open:	Apr-Sep, daily 0900-1700. Nov-Mar, daily 0900-dusk.
admission:	£4.25
description:	A beautiful four-acre garden designed for year-round interest through use of form, colour and texture. Beautiful plant centre, fully licensed Garden Cafe (Les Routiers approved).
facilities:	▣ 🎿 ⊼ ♿

High Beeches Woodland & Water Gardens

High Beeches Woodland & Water Gardens,
Handcross, RH17 6HQ **t:** (01444) 400589
w: highbeeches.com

open: Mar-Oct, Mon-Tue, Thu-Sun 1300-1700.
admission: £5.50

description: Twenty-five acres of peaceful, landscaped woodland and water gardens with many rare plants, wildflower meadow, spring bulbs and glorious autumn colour.

facilities: ▣ 🎿 ⊼ ♿

Nymans Garden

Nymans Garden, Handcross, RH17 6EB
t: (01444) 400321   **w:** nationaltrust.org.uk

open:	Mar-Dec, Wed-Sun 1100-1800.
admission:	£7.70

description:	A large romantic garden around the ruins of an old house with good views. Outstanding international collection of rare trees, shrubs and plants.

facilities: 🍽 🏹 ⛩ ♿

Borde Hill Garden

Borde Hill Garden, Balcombe Road, Haywards Heath, RH16 1XP   **t:** (01444) 450326
w: bordehill.co.uk

open:	Apr-Oct, daily 1000-1800.
admission:	£6.50

description:	Spring is heralded by magnificent magnolias, rhododendrons and azaleas, blending into summer with fragrant roses and herbaceous plants, followed by the rich colours of autumn.

facilities: 🍽 🐕 ⛩ ♿

Leonardslee Lakes and Gardens

LOWER BEEDING

Leonardslee Lakes and Gardens, Lower Beeding, RH13 6PP **t:** (01403) 891212 **w:** leonardslee.com

open: Apr-Oct, daily 0930-1800.
admission: £6.00

description: Rhododendrons and azaleas in 240-acre valley with seven lakes. Rock garden, bonsai, wallabies and wildfowl. Victorian motor cars and 1/12th scale country estate of 100 years ago.

facilities:

Uppark

PETERSFIELD

Uppark, South Harting, Petersfield, GU31 5QR
t: (01730) 825857 **w:** nationaltrust.org.uk

open: Apr-Oct, Mon-Thu, Sun 1230-1630.
admission: £7.50

description: Extensive exhibition shows the exciting work which restored this beautiful house and its treasures. Rescued paintings, ceramics and famous dolls' house. Nostalgic servants' rooms.

facilities:

West Dean Gardens

WEST DEAN

West Dean Gardens, West Dean, PO18 0QZ
t: (01243) 818210   **w:** westdean.org.uk

open:	Mar-Oct, 1030-1700. Nov-Feb, Wed-Sun 1030-1600.
admission:	£6.00

description: Highlights of this award-winning garden include a beautifully restored walled kitchen garden with Victorian glasshouses, extensive formal gardens, arboretum, pergola.

facilities: ♨ 🕺 🪑 ♿

Highdown Gardens

WORTHING

Highdown Gardens, Littlehampton Road, Highdown, Worthing, BN12 6PE   **t:** (01903) 221112   **w:** worthing.gov.uk

open: Apr-Sep, daily 1000-1800. Oct-Nov, Mon-Fri 1000-1630. Dec-Jan, Mon-Fri 1000-1600. Feb-Mar, 1000-1630.

description: A nine-acre chalk pit garden on a southern slope. Rock plants and flowering shrubs thriving on lime soil, rose garden and spring bulb collection including naturalised daffodils.

facilities: ♨ 🕺 ♿

ABERFORD

Lotherton Hall & Gardens

Lotherton Hall & Gardens, Aberford, LS25 3EB
t: (0113) 281 3259 **w:** leeds.gov.uk

open: House - Apr-Oct, Tue-Sat, 1000-1700, Sun 1300-1700. Nov, Dec, Mar, Tue-Sat 1000-1600, Sun 1200-1600. Garden - All year, Dawn-Dusk.

admission: £3.00

description: Edwardian gentleman's country house with formal Edwardian gardens including abundant herbaceous borders and a wildflower lawn. Paintings, furniture, silver, porcelain, 19thC and 20thC art. Deer park and bird garden.

facilities:

ADEL

York Gate Garden

York Gate Garden, Back Church Lane, Adel, LS16 8DW
t: (0113) 267 8240 **w:** perennial.org.uk

open: Apr-Sep, Thu, Sun, Bank Hols 1400-1700.

admission: £3.50

description: A one-acre garden created by the Spencer family between 1951 and 1994. It is recognised as one of the most innovative small gardens in the world.

facilities:

See pages 2-3 for key to symbols

Bramham Park

Bramham Park, Bramham, LS23 6ND
t: (01937) 846000

open:	Apr-Jul, Sep, daily 1130-1630.
admission:	£4.00

description: Bramham Park has been the home of the Lane
Fox family for 300 years. The house was built
in 1698 by Robert Benson, 1st Lord Bingley, in
the style of the great Tuscan villas he had seen
on a grand tour of Europe.

facilities: 🍵 🐕 🔼 ♿

Golden Acre Park

Golden Acre Park, Otley Road, Bramhope, LS16 8BQ
t: (0113) 395 7400   **w:** leeds.gov.uk

open: All year, daily.

description: Set in 179 acres of mature woodland
surrounding an attractive lake. Many varieties
of trees, shrubs and herbaceous plants.
Demonstration gardens, vegetables and
flowers. Wild flora encouraged around the
lake.

facilities: 🍵 🐕 🔼 ♿

Land Farm Garden

COLDEN

Land Farm Garden, Colden, HX7 7PJ
t: (01422) 842260

open: May-Aug, Sat-Sun, Bank Hols 1000-1700.
admission: £3.00

description: The five-acre gardens have been constructed entirely by the owner for ease of maintenance. The gardens are well known for their sculpture, meconopses, azaleas, rhododendrons and summer borders.

facilities:

BTCV Wildlife Garden

KIRKSTALL

BTCV Wildlife Garden, Hollybush Conservation Centre, Broad Lane, Kirkstall, LS5 3BP **t:** (0113) 274 2335 **w:** btcv.org.uk

open: All year, Mon-Fri 1300-1600.

description: The Hollybush Nature Garden has been created on a formerly derelict site and consists of many varied habitats, creating a haven for wildlife and an inspiration to visitors.

facilities:

See pages 2-3 for key to symbols

Hollies Botanical Garden

Hollies Botanical Garden, off Weetwood Lane, Leeds,
LS16 5NZ   **t:** (0113) 232 3069

open: All year, dawn-dusk.

description: Twenty-two hectares of
land comprising flowering
rhododendrons and azaleas
from early spring to summer, herbaceous
borders, mature plants and large woodland
walks on three different levels.

facilities: 🐕

Roundhay Park

Roundhay Park, Leeds, LS8 1ER
t: (0113) 266 1850   **w:** leeds.gov.uk

open: Daily.

description: One of Europe's largest municipal parks,
comprising over 700 acres of rolling parkland
with lakes, woodland, the gorge and ravine
and specialist gardens. It is also home to
Tropical World.

facilities: 🍽 🐕 🪑 ♿

Yorkshire Sculpture Park

WEST BRETTON

Yorkshire Sculpture Park, West Bretton, WF4 4LG
t: (01924) 832515 **w:** ysp.co.uk

open: Apr-Oct, daily 1000-1800. Nov-Mar, daily 1000-1700.

description: Set in the beautiful grounds of a 500-acre, 18thC country estate, the park is one of the world's leading open-air galleries and presents a changing programme of international sculpture exhibitions.

facilities:

Peto Garden

BRADFORD-ON-AVON

The Peto Garden, Iford Manor, Bradford-on-Avon, BA15 2BA
t: (01225) 863146 **w:** ifordmanor.co.uk

open: May-Sep, Tue-Thu, Sat-Sun 1400-1700.
admission: £4.50

description: Italianate garden created by Harold Peto. This romantic hillside garden is characterised by pools, terraces, sculptures, evergreen planting and rural views.

facilities:

Sheldon Manor Gardens

Sheldon Manor Gardens, Sheldon Manor, Chippenham, SN14 0RG **t:** (01249) 653120 **w:** sheldonmanor.co.uk

open:	Apr-Oct, Thu, Sun, Bank Hols 1400-1800.
admission:	£4.50

description: Sheldon Manor is Wiltshire's oldest inhabited manorhouse with a 13thC porch and a 15thC chapel. Gardens with ancient yews, a mulberry tree and a profusion of old-fashioned roses blooming in May and June.

facilities:

Courts

The Courts, Holt, BA14 6RR
t: (01225) 782340

open:	Apr-Oct, Mon-Tue, Thu-Sun 1100-1730.
admission:	£5.00

description: This delightful and tranquil seven-acre English country garden is full of charm, variety and colour with herbaceous borders, water gardens, topiary and arboretum.

facilities:

Lackham Country Park

LACOCK

Lackham Country Park, Wiltshire College Lackham, Lacock,
SN15 2NY   **t:** (01249) 466800
w: lackhamcountrypark.co.uk

open: Aug, Mon-Fri, Sun 1000-1700.
admission: £2.00

description: Idyllically situated in the
Wiltshire countryside. Discover formal
and historic walled gardens, a rural-life museum housed in
thatched buildings and woodland walks.

facilities:

Heale Garden & Plant Centre

MIDDLE WOODFORD

Heale Garden & Plant Centre, Middle Woodford, SP4 6NT
t: (01722) 782504   **w:** greatbritishgardens.co.uk

open:	Feb-Oct, Wed-Sun 1000-1630.
admission:	£4.00

description: Mature traditional garden with shrubs,
kitchen garden, musk and other roses.
Authentic Japanese teahouse in water garden.
Magnolias, snowdrops and aconites in winter.

facilities:

Stourhead House and Garden

Stourhead House and Garden, The National trust, The Estate Office, Stourton, BA12 6QD   **t:** (01747) 841152
w: nationaltrust.org.uk

open:	Garden: All year, daily 0900-1900. House: Apr-Oct, Mon-Tue, Fri-Sun 1130-1630.
admission:	£10.40
description:	Landscaped garden laid out c1741-80, with lakes, temples, rare trees and plants. House, begun c1721 by Colen Campbell, contains fine paintings and Chippendale furniture.
facilities:	☕ 🕴 🏕 ♿

Stourton House Flower Garden

Stourton House Flower Garden, Stourton House, Stourton, BA12 6QF   **t:** (01747) 840417

open:	Apr-Nov, Wed, Thu, Sun, Bank Hols 1100-1800. Open days: last 2 Sundays in Feb.
admission:	£3.50
description:	Garden of varied and colourful shrubs with hedged borders, delphinium and rose walks, ponds, woodland glades and secret garden. Magnificent feature hedge. Wild flowers encouraged. Unique collection of daffodils, 270 varieties of hydrangeas. Year-round col
facilities:	☕ 🕴 ♿

Larmer Tree Gardens

TOLLARD ROYAL

Larmer Tree Gardens, Tollard Royal,
SP5 5PT   **t:** (01725) 516225
w: larmertreegardens.co.uk

open:	Apr-Jun, Aug-Sep, Mon-Thu, Sun 1100-1630. Oct-Nov, Feb-Mar, Mon-Thu 1100-1630.
admission:	£3.75
description:	These historical gardens of General Pitt Rivers are the secret gardens of Wiltshire. Rare and unusual planting and exhibits of General Pitt Rivers' work. Regular concerts and festivals.
facilities:	

Arley Arboretum

BEWDLEY

Arley Arboretum, Arley, Bewdley, DY12 1SQ
t: (01299) 861368   **w:** arley-arboretum.org.uk

open: Apr-Oct, Wed-Sun, Bank Hols 1100-1700.
admission: £4.00

description: One of the oldest privately owned arboretums in the country with listed walled garden containing Italianate garden, herbaceous borders, picnic area, tea room and plant sales.

facilities:

Witley Court

Witley Court, Great Witley, WR6 6JT
t: (01299) 896636   **w:** english-heritage.org.uk

open:	Apr-May, Sep-Oct, Mar, daily 1000-1700. June-Aug, daily 1000-1700.Nov-Feb, Mon, Thu-Sun 1000-1600.
admission:	£5.20
description:	Spectacular ruins of one of England's great country houses surrounded by magnificent landscaped gardens designed by Nesfield, and featuring the great Perseus and Andromeda fountain.
facilities:	![icons]

Hanbury Hall (National Trust)

Hanbury Hall (National Trust), School Road, Hanbury, WR9 7EA   **t:** (01527) 821214   **w:** nationaltrust.org.uk

open:	Mar-Oct, Mon-Wed, Sat-Sun 1300-1700. Nov-Feb, Sat-Sun 1300-1700.
admission:	£6.80
description:	Beautiful English country house with tranquil 18thC gardens and views over 400 acres of parkland. Unusual features include outstanding murals, mushroom house and bowling green.
facilities:	![icons]

Eastgrove Cottage Garden Nursery

Eastgrove Cottage Garden Nursery, Sankyns Green, Nr Shrawley, Little Witley, WR6 6LQ   **t:** (01299) 896389
w: eastgrove.co.uk

open:	Apr, Thu-Sat, Bank Hols 1400-1700. May, Mon, Thu-Sun, Bank Hols 1400-1700. Jun, Thu-Sat, Bank Hols. Sep, Thu-Sat 1400-1700.
admission:	£4.00
description:	Old-world English cottage garden full of scent and colour in country setting. Plants for sale. Owners available for advice. An RHS Partnership garden.
facilities:	

Spetchley Park Gardens

Spetchley Park Gardens, Spetchley Park, Spetchley, WR5 1RS   **t:** (01453) 810303   **w:** spetchleygardens.co.uk

open:	Mar-Sep, Wed-Sun, Bank Hols 1100-1800. Oct, Sat-Sun 1100-1600.
admission:	£6.00
description:	The Gardens are amongst the finest in the country. Set in lovely countryside three miles east of Worcester, they extend over 30 acres and include many rare trees, shrubs and plants of interest, both to the professional gardener and to the amateur.
facilities:	

Stone House Cottage Gardens

Stone House Cottage Gardens, Stone, DY10 4BG
t: (01562) 69902   **w:** shcn.co.uk

open:	Apr-Sep, Wed-Sat 1000-1700.
admission:	£3.00

description: A very beautiful old walled garden with rare wall shrubs and climbers, herbaceous plants. In an adjacent nursery, there is a large selection of unusual plants for sale.

facilities: 🍴 ♿

Bodenham Arboretum

Bodenham Arboretum, Wolverley, DY11 5SY
t: (01562) 852444   **w:** bodenham-arboretum.co.uk

open:	Mar-Sep, Wed-Sun 1100-1700. Oct, daily 1100-1700. Nov-Dec, Wed-Sun 1100-1700. Jan-Feb, Sat-Sun 1100-1700.
admission:	£5.00
description:	This award winning arboretum, set within a working farm of 156 acres, contains over 2,700 species of trees and shrubs.

facilities: ☕ 🐕 🪧 ♿

Webbs of Wychbold, Garden Centre

 Webbs of Wychbold, Garden Centre, Wychbold, WR9 0DG   **t:** (01527) 860000
w: webbsofwychbold.co.uk

open: All year, Mon-Sat 0900-1800, Sun 1030-1630.

description: Fifty acres of gardening, leisure and pleasure. Inspirational riverside gardens, book, card and gift shop, vast range of plants and a relaxing cafe restaurant.

facilities: ▆ 🏃 🅰 ♿